# Sea-Arama Marineworld
# Galveston, Texas

By Tim Gould

Sea-Arama Marineworld Galveston, Texas
Copyright © 2016 Tim Gould
2nd Edition Copyright © 2018
All rights reserved.
Printed in the United States of America

Cover Design: Elaina Lee
Editor: Jenny Mertes

ISBN 13: 978-1537239552
ISBN 10: 1537239554

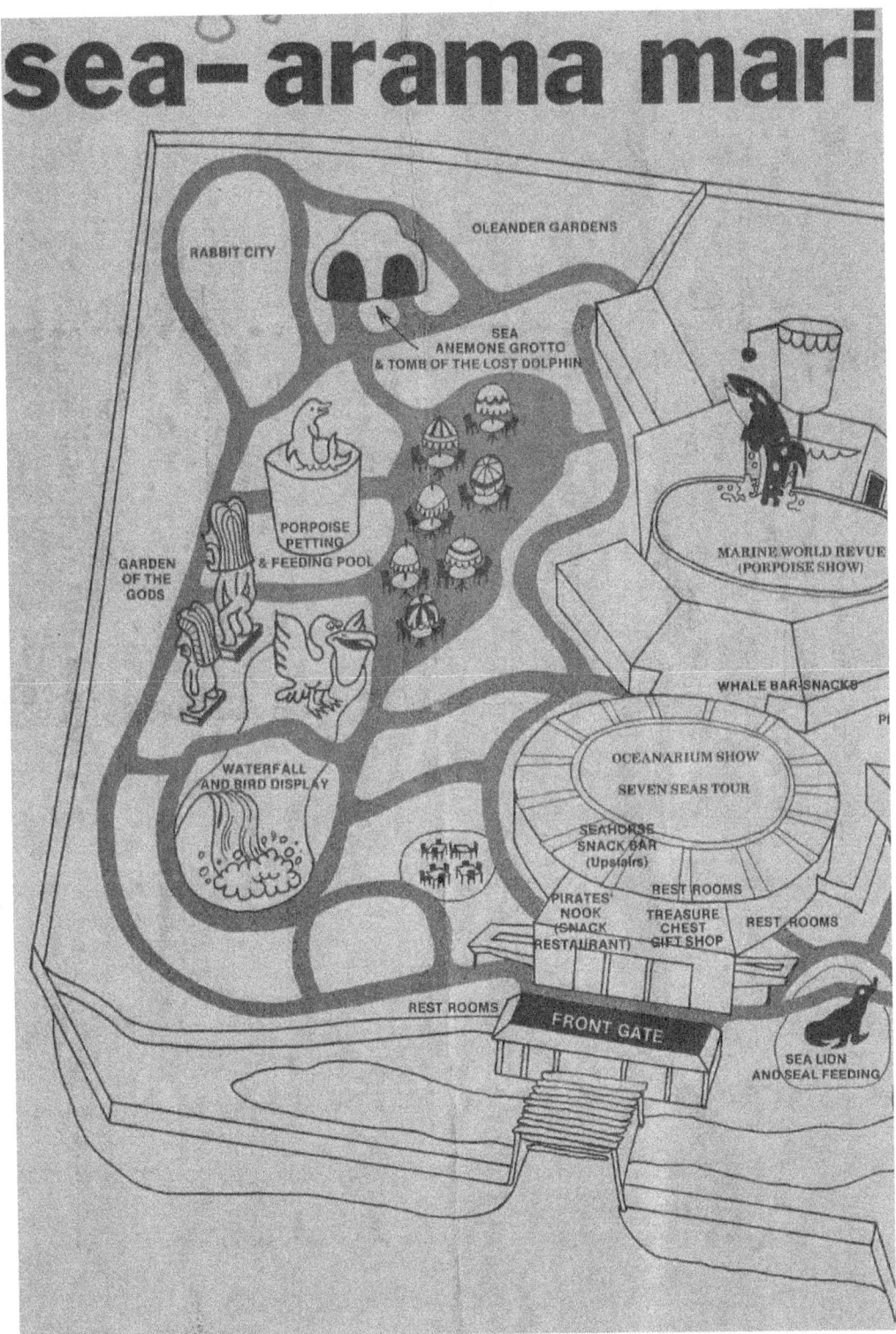

1974 Sea-Arama map. *Courtesy of Chris Barker.*

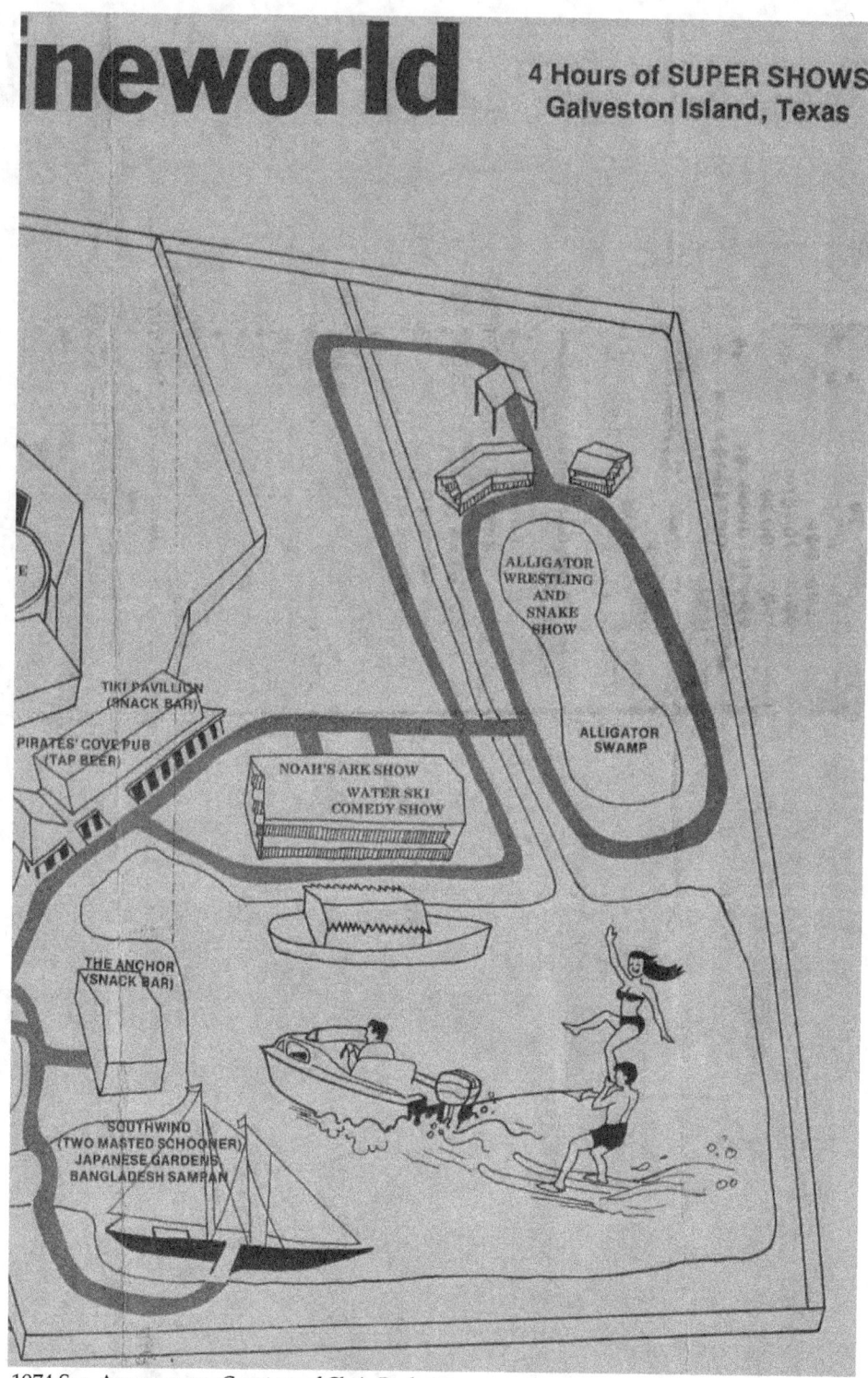

ineworld
**4 Hours of SUPER SHOWS**
**Galveston Island, Texas**

1974 Sea-Arama map. *Courtesy of Chris Barker.*

# Contents

# Title Page Photo Credits

Credits and descriptions of title page photos and illustrations:

**Alligators**–Ken Jones; *Courtesy of Krystal Knutson.* **Birds**–Amber Jinkins Shelley; *Courtesy of Krystal Knutson.* **Jungle Fantasy Wild Cat Show**–John Campolongo; *Author's collection.* **M.A.T.W.**–Ken Ramirez; *Courtesy of Russ O'Connor.* **Noah's Ark**–Judy Zaun; *Author's collection.* **Oceanarium and Jewel Tanks**–1980s Shark Adventure sign; *Courtesy of David Thibodeaux.* **Other Animal Exhibits**–Original drawing by trainer Doug Messinger; *Author's collection.* **Petting Zoo**–Petting Zoo sign; *Courtesy of David Thibodeaux.* **Pig Show**–Judy Zaun with performing pigs. *Courtesy of Judy Zaun.* **Porpoise/Dolphin Show**–Dolphins in back stage holding tank; *Courtesy of Russ O'Connor.* **Porpoise petting/feeding pool**–Porpoise petting/feeding pool; *Author's collection.* **Sea Lions and Seals**–Harbor Seal sign; *Courtesy of David Thibodeaux.* **Ski Show**–Nick O'Donohoe and Jackie Rourke; *Courtesy of Remembering Sea-Arama website.* **Snakes**–Jim Ketchum; *Courtesy of Ken Gray.* **Southwind Schooner**–Southwind at Sea-Arama; *Author's collection.* **Three Bears Show**–Judy Zaun; *Courtesy of Judy Zaun.* **Whales**–1989 Pacific Black Whale sign; *Courtesy of David Thibodeaux.* **Other Places in the Park**–Gift shop glass; *Courtesy of Remembering Sea-Arama website.* **Sea-Arama Marineworld Publicity**–Restaurant table advertisement; *Courtesy of Krystal Knutson.* **Marine Mammal Stranding Network**–Dolphins Lucky and Hastings; *Author's collection.*

**1965**–Original façade and landscaping; *Courtesy of James P. Kelly Jr.* **1966**–Kathryn McDonald kissing sea lion; *Courtesy of Kathryn (Kathy) McDonald Taubert & digitization, courtesy of Robert Cubbage.* **1967**–Lafitte the porpoise; *Courtesy of James P. Kelly Jr.* **1968**–Penguins in the Porpoise Show; *Author's collection.* **1969**–Oceanarium Dive to the Deep; *Courtesy of James P. Kelly Jr.* **1970**–Seal feeding; *Courtesy of Remembering Sea-Arama website.* **1971**–Mamuk Killer Whale Show; *Courtesy of Helen Varner.* **1972**–Sea-Arama Shark Bumper Sticker; *Author's collection.* **1973**–Dolphin tower hoop jump; *Courtesy of Krystal Knutson.* **1974**–Hal Newsom in the alligator show; *Courtesy of Hal Newsom.* **1975**–Galveston guidebook; *Author's collection.* **1976**–Camporee patch; *Author's collection.* **1977**–Hal Newsom, volunteer, Cuddles the Boa; *Courtesy of Helen Varner.* **1978**–Dolphin Show; *Courtesy of Craig Caskey.* **1979**–John Campolongo in the Jungle Fantasy Wild Cat Show; *Courtesy of Hal Newsom.* **1980**–Mike Cromie's employee badge; *Courtesy of Mike Cromie.* **1981**–Sea-Arama shark patch; *Courtesy of Tim Cromie.* **1982**–Sea-Arama sea lion patch; *Courtesy of Tim Cromie.* **1983**–Sea-Arama dolphins patch; *Courtesy of Tim Cromie.* **1984**–Galveston jail picture spot; *Courtesy of Remembering Sea-Arama website.* **1985**–Sea-Arama bumper sticker; *Courtesy of Greg May.* **1986**–Sea-Arama shark picture spot; *Courtesy of Clint Uselton.* **1987**–Gini Brown Sea-Arama business card; *Courtesy of Gini Brown.* **1988**–Sea-Arama discount coupon; *Courtesy of Gini Brown.* **1989**–Doug Lawrence with Sea Hag; *Courtesy of Doug Lawrence.* **1990**–Sea-Arama brochure featuring Cheryl Snyder Messinger; *Author's collection.* **Additional Sea-Arama Marineworld Employees**–Terry Moore in the ski show; *Courtesy of Tim Cromie.* **Sea-Arama Marineworld Stories**–Original "Remembering Sea-Arama" Website; *Courtesy of Remembering Sea-Arama website.* **2012 Sea-Arama Marineworld Employee Reunion**–3-foot by 5-foot entrance poster used at the reunion; *Author's collection.* **Sea-Arama Marineworld's Epilogue**–Sea-Arama in 2003; *Courtesy of Bob Ford Productions.*

# Acknowledgements

I want to say "thank you" to all who have given permission, either in the past or the present, to use their photos, stories, and documents, and thanks to all whom I interviewed. This book would not have been possible without all of you:

James P. Kelly Jr, Greg May, Krystal Knutson, Judy Zaun, Paul Ware, Kathryn McDonald Taubert, Steve O'Donohoe, Kevin Colston, Jim Dobberstine, Terry Moore, Kelli Jones, Mary Jo Urbani, Russ O'Connor, Brandy Smith, Hollis Danvers, Hal Newsom, Gini Brown, Tom Whitman, Ken Beggs, Ken Ramirez, Amy Ellison, Gin Thom, Tim Cromie, Mike Millard, Jovana Ivastanin, Bob Ford, John Masters, Hajare Family, and the *Galveston Daily News*–permission given by Michael Smith, May 23, 2016.

My apologies to anyone who may have been left off a list or whose name or information is incorrect; every attempt was made to be accurate.

Thank you to my editor, Jenny Mertes, who gave of her time and talents in the editing and polishing of this book.

# Introduction

I worked at Sea-Arama Marineworld in the late 1980s as a dolphin and sea lion trainer and show performer. I also performed in the bird shows occasionally.

In 2004 I decided to Google "Sea-Arama" and found nothing. This was long before there was Facebook or Flickr or any other website that had Sea-Arama information. I was disappointed that the world had forgotten about Sea-Arama and decided to do something about it.

In February 2005 I gathered all my photos and created a website called *Remembering Sea-Arama* at www.seaarama.zoomshare.com. I got Google and Yahoo and other search engines to show it in their top five results, and then I got the word out to every person, website, and e-mail I could about this new site. Eventually the *Galveston Newspaper, Galveston Monthly Magazine,* and *Houston Chronicle* published numerous stories on Sea-Arama and the original website. One of those articles was about the Sea-Arama Employee Reunion I went on to organize in 2012. The reunion took place at Galveston's Moody Gardens Aquarium Pyramid, and, with the help of Greg Whittaker, it was a huge success with more than 130 people attending.

In 2014 the free web provider I was using began to charge a fee, so I moved the website to its current location at www.seaarama.com or http://galveston.wix.com/rememberingseaarama. The website shows many more pictures than could be included in this book and offers numerous videos of Sea-Arama shows and news reports.

Today if you do a Google search for Sea-Arama, you'll not only find my website and Facebook page about Sea-Arama, you'll also find many other web and image results as well. I'm happy to see a renewed interest in Sea-Arama and feel like I was a part of that happening.

Tim Gould (AKA Wes)

Author's Note: This book follows the early Sea-Arama pattern of calling the dolphins "porpoises," calling the orcas "Killer Whales," and describing the animals doing "tricks" instead of behaviors. As the years passed, the terminology changed, so the latter part of this book uses the more accurate, updated terminology.

# Sea-Arama Marineworld Beginnings

Construction of Sea-Arama Marineworld. *Courtesy of James P. Kelly Jr.*

Sea-Arama Marineworld, a marine animal park in Galveston, Texas, opened in 1965 and was touted as the first of its kind between the east and west coasts. In 1937 Marineland of Florida had opened as the first oceanarium, which was the name given to an aquarium that displayed sea life in near-natural surroundings. This park was followed by another oceanarium in 1954, Marineland of the Pacific. In 1964 Hawaii's Sea Life Park, the Aquatarium in Florida, and SeaWorld in San Diego all opened their doors. The first two were copies of the originals and, at its opening, SeaWorld had only a few porpoises, sea lions, and attractions.

Sea-Arama was unique. No other park in America housed three separate and distinct features: an oceanarium, an aquarium, and a 1,000-seat aqua-amphitheater. It was also the first to have a porpoise show pool that was lined with glass panels, now a common sight at marine mammal parks. It was also the only major marine park between the east and west coasts to have a resident whale (Nemo the Pilot Whale).

Galveston was already a tourist destination because of its beaches, but the idea for a major oceanarium was created in 1957 by a group of Texas businessmen (Jack Dismukes in Austin). The original corporation was formed in October 1957, and many acres of land were acquired on the west side of the island around 91st Street in Galveston in 1960.

In 1961, technical and economic feasibility studies were done, and the businessmen chose a specific site at 91st Street and Seawall Boulevard. Galveston was ideal for the park's location because of its proximity to natural sea life and salt water, its accessibility to the greater Houston area, and the cooperation of Galveston's citizens and city government. Galveston city leaders had recognized the need for the island to extend its tourist season beyond the summer months, and so they helped to develop Sea-Arama as the first of several projects designed to boost year-round tourism on the island.

Groundbreaking was held in April 1964, and construction of Sea-Arama began in late 1964 on 38 acres (sometimes listed as 25 or 40) of land. The design of the park was done by Austin architectural firm Winfred O. Gustafson, and construction of the structures was overseen by engineer Kenneth E. Zimmerman, who also did the Warwick Hotel, Astrodome, Jesse Jones Hall for Performing Arts, UT Graduate School of Business, and Texas A&M's Olsen Stadium. With the assistance of technical experience and knowledge from Marineland of Florida, Sea-Arama was able to avoid many of the usual new park problems. In July 1965 a new corporation was formed by a merger from the old corporation.

The official opening occurred on November 7, 1965 (not November 8, as is sometimes reported). The overall cost was estimated at $2 million. The park opened to great fanfare, with 2,000 people attending. This larger-than-expected crowd meant that Sea-Arama had to put on four porpoise shows instead of the two that were planned, since the Porpoise Theater only seated 1,000. Admission was $2.25 for adults and $1.75 for students.

From that November opening until the next summer, Sea-Arama consisted of an oceanarium, aquariums, a gift shop, a camera shop, and a 200,000-gallon Porpoise Theater. Two different live shows were presented during that first year: the porpoise show and one in the Oceanarium, with over fifty species of the ocean's larger and more dangerous fish, including sharks, rays, barracudas, giant spotted groupers, Warsaw groupers, and sea turtles. Several times a day, a diver descended into the 160,000 (advertised as 170,000 or 200,000) gallon salt water tank to hand feed them.

The Oceanarium was circular, and lining its outer walls were twenty-eight aquarium tanks (called Jewel tanks) that were divided equally between fresh water and salt water exhibits. Later there would be 12 salt water and 16 fresh water exhibits. The fresh water exhibits included Texas game fish, archer fish, deadly piranha, an electric eel, and many fresh water tropical fish. The salt water exhibit included such specimens as butterfly fish, seahorses, vicious moray eels, lion fish, trigger fish, and all types of beautiful reef fish from the waters of the Atlantic and Pacific oceans. Almost every known family of fish was represented either in the Oceanarium or in the aquariums.

Attendance for the first ten months (November 1965–August 1966) was an impressive 200,000. In those first ten months, over 9,000 students visited the park. Sea-Arama was off and running, employing 33 full-time workers. After its first two years in existence, Sea-Arama was rated as one of the best aquariums in the world by oceanographers.

Completed Sea-Arama in 1966. Note the sea lion pool bottom right and the snack bar bottom left. *Courtesy of James P. Kelly Jr.*

# Shows and Exhibits

Beautiful Entrance to Fabulous Sea-Arama Marineworld

*An All Tom Corp. postcard, author's collection.*

# Alligators

## Alligator Display (East of front entrance)
**Feb/Mar 1968–July 1969**

## Alligator Wrestling Show
**May 1968–1976**

## Alligator Island/Swamp
**July 1969–1990**

Sea-Arama began acquiring alligators for the original display in January of 1968. It was located just east of the main entrance and in later years become the seal and sea lion display. Sometimes the animal acquisitions occurred so quickly that the facility wasn't ready for them. In January a 200-pound black alligator arrived from Lufkin before its enclosure was ready, and four more alligators had already been ordered. While waiting for its tank to be constructed, the black alligator had to live in a wooden crate.

The alligator wrestling show opened to the public in May 1968 after a press preview show was presented the previous month. At that time, the display included ten American alligators and one crocodile. The alligator show got started because spectators were amused by handlers poking around the original alligator exhibit. The display was very muddy and therefore it was dangerous for the handlers to interact with the alligators. Once the new Alligator Island and swamp were built, the handlers could get in the water and safely interact with them.

By May 1969 the alligator wrestling show had become one of the park favorites. The show included "putting the alligator to sleep" by putting the reptile on its back, which was an unnatural position for the animal. Another trick was holding the animal's jaw shut with the trainer's chin. Other visitor favorites were when the alligators snapped their tails and sent the sticks the trainers held into the crowd. The show ended with a laugh as the trainer picked up a small alligator to show to the crowd and for them to pet. Then the trainer would suddenly growl and move it toward someone in the crowd to scare them.

In July 1969 Sea-Arama opened its new Alligator Island (east of the Ski Stadium), which was also the new location for the alligator wrestling show. The island measured approximately 7,500 square feet and had divided ponds to accommodate the twenty-five alligators and three crocodiles. It was designed for half of the new home to be the show area and the other half to be a marshy natural environment, with the hopes that in this habitat they would mate as well as give the public the best view of these animals. The show part of this display included educational and interesting facts about the reptiles, and it had a 600-seat stadium. The new ponds were smooth so that the skin on the alligators' feet wouldn't rub off on the sides and bottom. This had been a problem in the original display, and sand had been put down to keep them from losing their skin.

In 1970 a snake show was added to the alligator show. The combination of the two shows proved to be a hit with audiences for many years. The alligator part of the show was a topsy-turvy match between man and 400-pound beasts that included tail lashing and jaw snapping. Overall, the alligator wrestling show was a visitor favorite, leaving many kids who grew up in the '60s with vivid memories of the brave alligator wrestlers straddling a 13-foot alligator—believed to be the largest living alligator in captivity in Texas at the time.

Prelude to Alligator Wrestling

*An All Tom Corp. postcard, author's collection.*

Howard Picard wrestling alligator in 1969. *Courtesy of Krystal Knutson.*

# Birds

**White Pelican Display** (East of entrance)
Aug 1969–1975?

**Brown Pelican Display** (West of entrance)
1976–1990

**Coastal/Exotic Bird Display** (West of main entrance by waterfall)
Feb 1970–1990

**Bird Show** (Part of Noah's Ark Show)
1975–May 1976

**Bird Show** (By itself)
June 1976–1990

Birds first appeared at Sea-Arama after the alligators were moved to their new island location. The old alligator site was turned into a seal and sea lion display, with a few white pelicans that had been injured and were recovering until released. The plan was to have many exotic birds there, but soon after, the birds ended up at the new lagoon and waterfall location on the west side of the park. This west side location would also become the location for the brown pelicans until the park closed.

Birds used in the shows didn't arrive until the end of the Noah's Ark show around 1975. At that time the birds were riding roller skates, shooting cannons, and riding bicycles on high wires. When the Noah's Ark show was eliminated, the birds got their own show using the stadium where the alligator wrestling show had just ended its run.

This is when the new pirate ship prop was built and subsequently used for the bird show until 1990. Eventually a new stadium was built in the same general location for the birds and other shows to use. The bird show would remain at this location until the park closed. The exception to this was during the winter when the bird show was taken inside the Oceanarium on the first floor.

In the 1980s the bird show was the "Parrot Pirate Melodrama" with Captain Harvey, the greater sulphur-crested cockatoo. Visitors could see him saving the day along with his macaw mates—Sea Hag, Peg Leg Pete, Butch, Little Red Beard, and Ahab, holding claws, riding roller skates, racing for peanuts, and yelling "Help!" in a Southern accent.

Endangered bird species became a major project at Sea-Arama. The park spent several years attempting to establish an actual breeding colony of brown pelicans. These birds were once a common site along the Texas coast. The program originally began in cooperation with the Florida-based Sunco Seabird Sanctuary and Shell Oil in 1976. The first 36 pelicans involved in the breeding program were tagged with identifiable leg markers when they came from southern Florida. Each year in the spring a small flock of the birds would fly from the park and then return in the winter, with the number of birds never changing. Eventually, untagged birds began returning to the park, leading curators to believe that the protected birds were breeding outside the park. Also, there was evidence that the birds might be nesting at the park itself.

White and brown pelicans were once endangered, but thanks in part to Sea-Arama they made a comeback and were moved from the endangered to the threatened category.

Harvey the Cockatoo in 1986. *Courtesy of Russ O'Connor.*

Brown pelicans in 1985. *Courtesy of John Masters.*

Roseate Spoonbills in 1986. *Courtesy of Russ O'Connor.*

Peacock in 1986. *Courtesy of Russ O'Connor.*

Tim Gould

Black Swans in 1986.
*Courtesy of Russ O'Connor.*

Roller skating macaw.
*Courtesy of Krystal Knutson.*

Bird show as part of Noah's
Ark Show. *Photo Stan Begam,
courtesy Dale Ware Family.*

Brown Pelican release/re-establish program mid to late 1970s. Back Row: Judy Zaun? unknown, Dale Ware, Ken Beggs, unknown. By Crate: Fred Colorado, unknown, Jimmy Watson. *Courtesy of Dale Ware Family Archives.*

Macaw on bike. *Courtesy of Greg May.* Macaws on bird show stage in 1986. *Courtesy of Russ O'Connor.*

# Jungle Fantasy Wild Cat Show
## Nov 1978–May 1981

In 1978 John Campolongo joined Sea-Arama with his "Jungle Fantasy Wild Cat Show." The actual start date of this show was November 6, 1978, rather than the advertised dated of Thanksgiving week. The show ran on weekends at the park until the spring of 1979, when it was done daily during the summer. In 1980 the show was done two times per day in April and three times per day during the summer.

Campolongo was already known for his big cat shows around the world, and when he started the show at Sea-Arama his animals included Ravi, a 400-pound Bengal tiger; Sabra, a 185-pound Asian leopard; Kunta, a 140-pound black panther; and Duke, a 73-pound German shepherd dog. At the time of opening, his hope was to add a male lion, polar bear, and cougar to the show in the near future.

Campolongo's wild animals were trained to perform behaviors that were unique to each animal. The show was fast moving because Campolongo didn't take time for bows. He entered the show area with no protection and was assisted only by Miss Sharon Little, a professional dancer turned trainer who later became his wife.

Each animal was dangerous in its own way. The leopard had the worst character, because in the wild they slept by day and stalked victims by night. This animal was strong enough to carry off a bull. The black panther was the least trustworthy and could easily become too excited. The tiger was strong enough to clear a seven-foot fence, cover 20 feet in a single bound, climb trees, or swim if it wanted to. During the show Campolongo would say to the animals, "Okay you guys, pay attention." He had developed a unique rapport with each animal that went beyond the usual trainer-animal relationship. In the show the animals would walk a high wire, jump, roll barrels, and jump through a ring of fire.

John Campolongo. *Courtesy of Sharon Campolongo.*

Sharon Campolongo with baby cougar Chuka.
*Courtesy of Krystal Knutson.*

# Marine Animal Training Workshop
## 1974–1990

The Marine Animal Training Workshop (M.A.T.W.) made its appearance at Sea-Arama in 1974 and lasted until the park closed.

The show consisted of educating the public on how training was done with the animals by explanation and example.

By the late 1980s the show was done exclusively with dolphins and involved one trainer announcing the show and one trainer working with the dolphin. The dolphin would perform various behaviors that it knew, some that the audience would see in the shows and some they would not.

While not as flashy as some of the other shows, it achieved its purpose of explaining operant conditioning, revealing the intelligence of the animals, and helping the audience to connect more with the animals.

Tim Gould and Hastings in 1989 during the M.A.T.W. *Author's collection.*

# Noah's Ark
## May 1972–May 1976

Sea-Arama had a large ski lake that was used during the summer for the ski show. The park wanted to utilize the stadium year-round, so they came up with the idea of a show on a boat. This show got its name because it was performed on a floating stage that faced the 1,500-seat ski stadium.

The actual start date was May 15, 1972, even though it was scheduled to start June 1, 1971. The reason it was delayed was that trainer Bob Landers had a difficult time putting the animals together on the ark. He had to figure out a way to not only hold the animals' attention, but also keep the sea lions, penguins, and elephant seal from diving into the lake and swimming off in search of food. He spent over 14 months working on solving these problems before the show could be presented.

The trainer played Noah while Fat Albert (an elephant seal) was his helper. The show was about all the problems "Fats" had in organizing all the animals.

Various animals were used throughout the show's run, including Leaperace the kangaroo, who played the piano, Rocky the raccoon, a pig named Archie Bunker that kept the beaches clean, and another pig named Arnold that ran onto the stage with a sign tied to his tail that read "The End." In 1975 a swimming pig was added, according to newspaper advertisements. Also participating were Heidi the sea lion, penguins named Nixon, Agnew, and Johnson, a pelican, a donkey, Flippo the monkey, Pepe the skunk, sea gulls, sheep, goats, and a coatimundi.

In addition to these animals, the last few years of the show included exotic birds doing tricks such as roller-skating. One of the bird stars was a cockatoo that appeared on the TV show *Baretta*. But the star of the show was Fat Albert. He had arrived from Marine World in Redwood City, California in November 1972.

The ark was docked on the west side of the ski lake by the sea lion pool, and they would use the sea lions in that pool for the Noah's Ark show. The ark was pulled by a winch into the performing location of the lake, and this made the ark a constant problematic setting. It had to be winched in and out of position to accommodate the ski show in the summer, and that winch would often break down.

Sea lion in the Noah's Ark show. *Courtesy of Krystal Knutson.*

Coatimundi in the Noah's ark show. *Courtesy of Krystal Knutson.*

Leaperace, the piano playing kangaroo will entertain you.

Judy Zaun with kangaroo and raccoon. *Author's collection.*

Judy Zaun with Noah's Ark raccoon. *Courtesy of Judy Zaun.*

Judy Zaun with Noah's Ark donkey. *Courtesy of Judy Zaun.*

Judy Zaun with Noah's Ark kangaroo. *Courtesy of Judy Zaun.*

Sea gulls in the Noah's Ark Show. *Astrocard Co. postcard, author's collection.*

Judy Zaun and Harvey during the Noah's Ark Show. *Photo by Stan Begam, courtesy of Judy Zaun.*

# Oceanarium and Jewel Tanks
## 1965–1990

**Dive to the Deep Show** (called "Oceanarium Show" in '73, '74)
1965–1980

**Seven Seas Tour**
1967–1990

**Mermaid/Scuba Show**
1968–1981

**Mermaid and Shark Show**
May 1975–Apr 1976

**Alice in Waterland (Mermaid Show)**
1976?–1979?

**Shark Exhibit**
1977–?

**Shark Adventure Show** (with cage)
Feb 1981–1990

The 160,000-gallon Oceanarium was the original crown jewel of Sea-Arama. The park was the first to have a covered or roofed oceanarium, which gave greater control over water conditions in the Oceanarium. An eight-inch saltwater line ran through the Galveston seawall about six feet below the surface of the boulevard, supplying salt water to the Oceanarium and the 32 tanks of marine specimens.

One of the park's first shows was the "Dive to the Deep Show." This show, along with the porpoise show, would be there at the beginning and end of the park's life. Visitors would make their way up the cement ramps into the second floor of the Oceanarium. Once inside the darkened halls, they could see through the thirty-two viewing ports that were eight feet under water. The Oceanarium held different varieties of salt water fish throughout the years, including a variety of sharks, large stingrays, moray eels, seals, groupers, exotic barracudas, and sawfish. During Dive to the Deep, visitors watched as divers entered and fed the many dangerous creatures.

Soon after Dive to the Deep began, another show started inside the Oceanarium. The "Seven Seas Tour" took the visitors around the outside wall of the Oceanarium floor to look at the decorated aquariums, called jewel tanks. A twenty-minute narrative accompanied the tour and introduced visitors to some of the most exotic and rarest fresh water and salt water fish in the world. The number of these jewel tanks varied over the years, from 22 to 28. A variety of fresh and salt water fish were kept in them throughout the park's life, including the deadly stone fish, Australia's colorful lion fish, South America's dangerous piranha, and the Texas exhibit featuring 27 varieties of native fish.

A few years after Dive to the Deep began in the Oceanarium, mermaids were added to the show. In what was also known as the SCUBA show, female swimmers frolicked under water among 400 dangerous sea creatures as divers entered the tank to feed the man-eaters. Both the mermaids and the divers not only fed the animals, but also demonstrated diving equipment and showed what can happen to divers below the surface.

One of the mermaids, Judy Zaun, said that in 1973 Barnaby the Harbor seal started in the Oceanarium with her. She trained him to swim with her during the mermaid routine, waving at viewers and kissing the glass.

The 1976 brochure listed the show as the "Oceanarium Shark-Mermaid Show," but by the 1980s the mermaids were no longer included, and a new diver cage had been put into the water of the Oceanarium. A diver would be in the cage surrounded by 500-pound sharks, which were in a feeding frenzy. The bars of the cage were just wide enough for the sharks to partially insert their heads and gaping mouths. From underwater, the diver talked to the audience assembled at the viewing windows.

Many of Sea-Arama's bull sharks were from the Gulf of Mexico and were caught by William "Buzz" Sinclair.

The Dive to The Deep Show

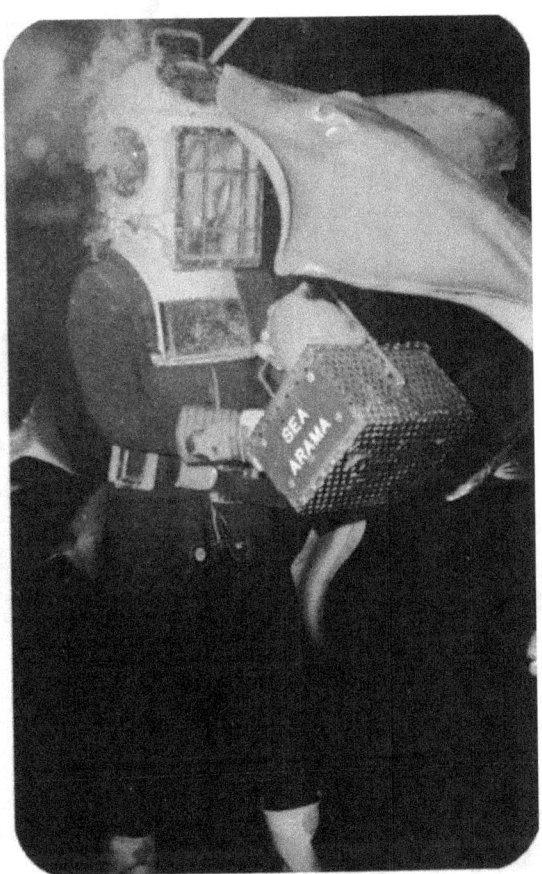

Sea-Arama Diver's Cage. (Pictured at the 2012 Reunion at Moody Gardens Aquarium Pyramid). *Courtesy of Krystal Knutson.*

*An All Tom Corp. postcard, author's collection.*

Jewel tank in the Oceanarium, ca. 1986. *Courtesy of Russ O'Connor.*

Tim Gould

Oceanarium with "mermaids." *An All Tom Corp. postcard, author's collection.*

Queen Angle

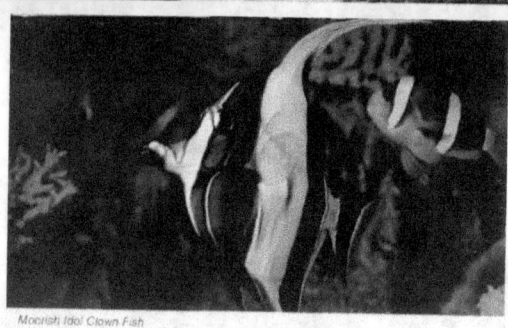

Moorish Idol Clown Fish

Jewel tank fish. *Author's collection.*

Jewel tank in 1986. *Courtesy of Russ O'Connor.*

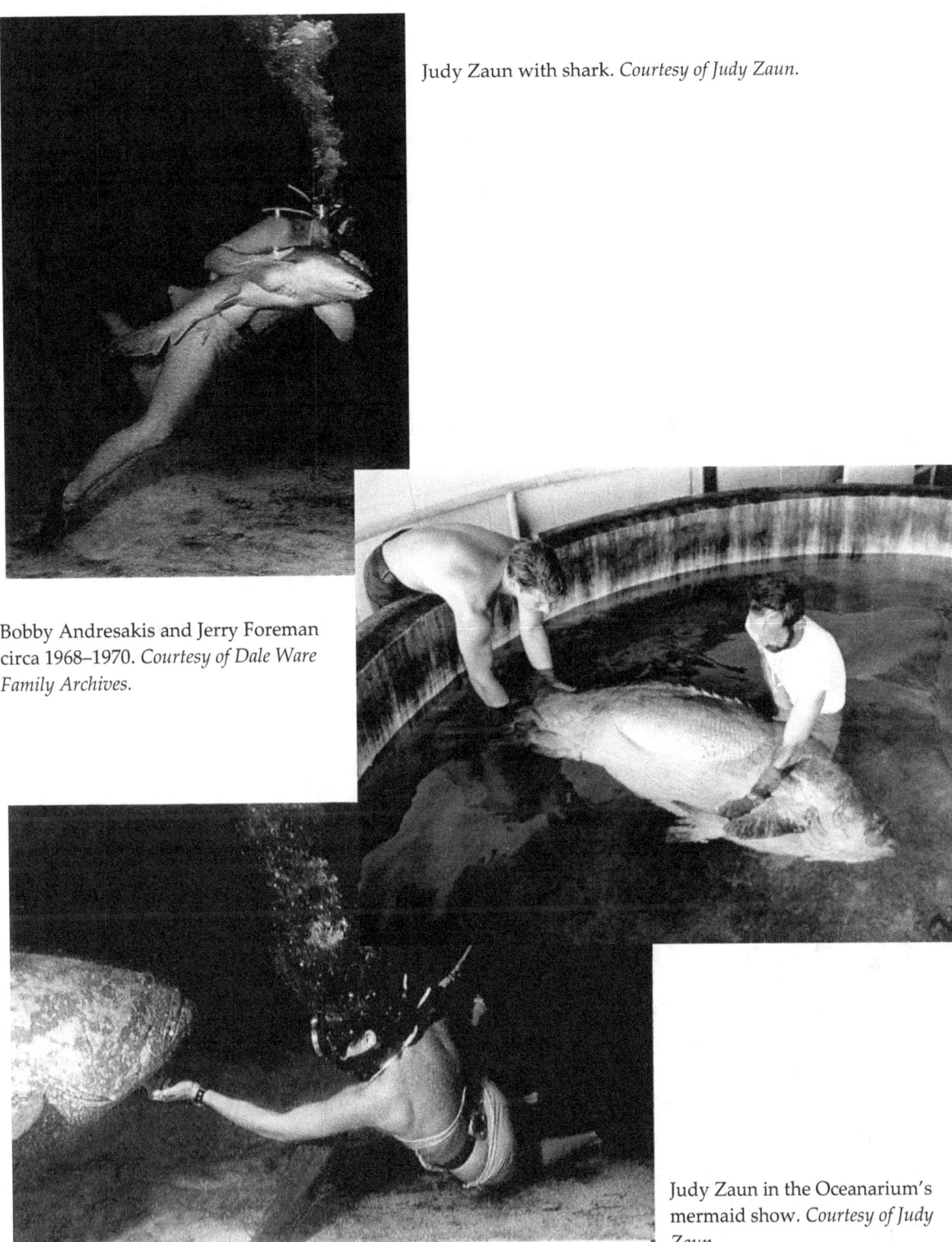

Judy Zaun with shark. *Courtesy of Judy Zaun.*

Bobby Andresakis and Jerry Foreman circa 1968–1970. *Courtesy of Dale Ware Family Archives.*

Judy Zaun in the Oceanarium's mermaid show. *Courtesy of Judy Zaun*

# Other Animal Exhibits

### Penguins
### Nov 1967–1975 & 1976?

### Octopus Grotto (Octopus, sea anemones, Tomb of the Lost Dolphin)
### Aug 1968–1971

### Aldabra Tortoises
### Mid/Late 1970s?–1990

Sea-Arama had a wide variety of animals that included both marine and non-marine mammals.

Penguins were introduced early in the park's history, participating in the Marineworld Porpoise Revue before making their way to the Noah's Ark Show. In the 1970s they had their own exhibit on the west side of the ski lake, where they could be observed when not performing in a show.

The Octopus Grotto was opened in 1968 and was designed to be a completely different experience. Visitors entered the grotto through a cave-like door and made their way through the darkened halls to get to the underwater viewing area. There they could view Ollie, a giant Atlantic octopus, in his 1,000-gallon tank. A ten-minute narration explained interesting facts about his home and habits. For its time, this attraction was cutting edge.

In 1970 the Sea Anemone display was added to the Octopus Grotto, allowing the public to hold and closely examine the flower-like sea creatures.

The Tomb of the Lost Dolphin was another new display added to the Octopus Grotto in 1970. A dolphin had beached itself on West Galveston Island in 1969 and was brought to Sea-Arama for care before it died. It was a rough-toothed dolphin usually found only in the Indian Ocean. Because of its rarity, Sea-Arama decided to preserve the animal through taxidermy and display the animal's skeleton, a fiberglass reproduction, and a narration telling the story behind the animal.

Ollie the octopus was stolen in 1971 and another one was obtained, with a third one reported to have been ordered for the exhibit. In 1975 the grotto was turned into the Amazon River Grotto, with piranhas replacing the octopus.

Sometime in the mid to late 1970s the park acquired the giant Aldabra land tortoises, one of the largest species of tortoise. The animals were related to the Galapagos Island tortoises but were from the Seychelles Island. They were enormous, with a shell length that measured more than 49 inches. These tortoises could grow to more than 400 pounds and live up to 150 years.

Another project that began in the early 1980s was the raising of the endangered Ridley sea turtle. The National Oceanic and Atmospheric Administration (NOAA) partnered with the park in conducting studies on the growth and feeding habits of the turtles at Sea-Arama.

There were monkeys and apes at the park, some of which were in the Noah's Ark Show, including Flippo the monkey. There was also a gibbon named Harpo as well as Annie the chimpanzee.

Octopus Grotto, ca. 1968. *Courtesy of Krystal Knutson.*

Aldabra tortoise enclosure. *Courtesy of Greg May.*

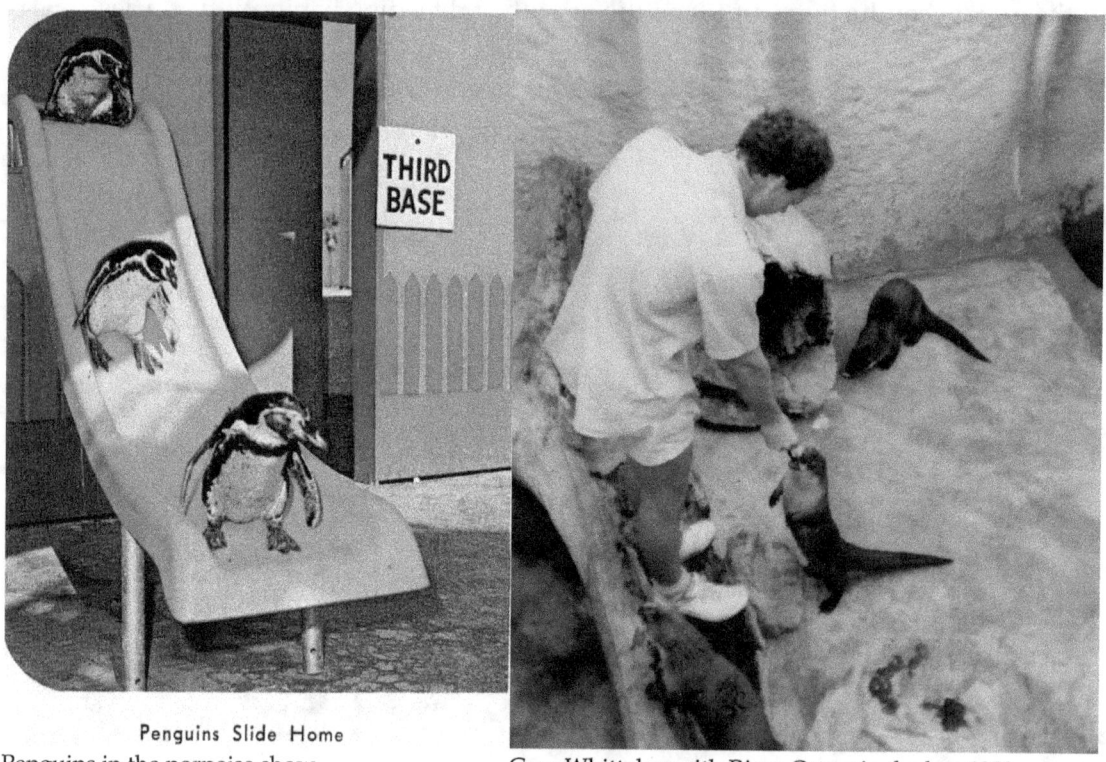

Penguins in the porpoise show.
*An All Tom Corp. postcard, author's collection.*

Greg Whittaker with River Otters in the late 1980s.
*Courtesy of Jim Dobberstine.*

# Petting Zoo

## June 1970–Feb 1979

This exhibit was originally called a deer petting park. The intention was to have fallow deer, Peruvian llamas, and other domestic animals for children to feed and pet. By 1973 it was being listed on the Sea-Arama maps as "Rabbit City and small animals" and then in 1974 it was listed simply as "Rabbit City." Then on the 1975 map it was listed as "Petting Zoo." The 1976 brochure lists wallabies, gigantic turtles, and deer in the "Wildlife Compound."

Petting Zoo goat. *Courtesy of Krystal Knutson.*

Petting Zoo enclosure. *Courtesy of David Thibodeaux.*

Alice Law and Debbie Murray with Petting Zoo lamb in 1977. *Courtesy of Krystal Knutson.*

# Pig Show
## 1978 & 1979?

Sea-Arama had a pig show for at least one year in 1978. The pigs got their start at Sea-Arama in the Noah's Ark show. Then, when the bear show ended in October 1977, the training staff decided to add a pig show as another land animal act. The park acquired three more pigs and did the show in the alligator stadium. Some of the pigs' names were Pork, Beans, Oscar, and Meyer. Thanks to Judy Zaun for a look at these rare photos of this brief show.

Judy Zaun in the Pig Show. *Courtesy of Judy Zaun.*

Judy Zaun in the Pig Show. *Courtesy of Judy Zaun.*

Judy Zaun in the Pig Show. *Courtesy of Judy Zaun.*

# Porpoise/Dolphin Show
## 1965–1990

The Marineworld Revue Porpoise Show was one of the original shows when the park opened, and it was one of the shows still remaining when the park closed.

Today, similar shows can be found in many different parks. But in the mid-1960s they were still something of a novelty.

When the park opened in 1965, the overwhelming number of park visitors meant that more porpoise shows had to be scheduled. The visitors to this show were delighted to see high-jumping, tandem pole jumping, putting out a fire, collecting and carrying hoops, a trio "singing" number, bowing to the audience, a baseball game that included two trainers and two porpoises, a football passing routine, walking backwards, and other tricks.

By January of 1966 Sea-Arama was already thinking of how to improve and expand the park, which already included the popular Marineworld Revue Porpoise Show. At that time there were no sea lions in the shows or on exhibit, but Heidi, the first sea lion at Sea-Arama, was being taught tricks by trainer Teeny Kelly and others in preparation for inclusion in the porpoise show. By April 1967, the sea lions Farouk and Heidi were finally part of the porpoise show.

Sometimes the park would present a special Christmas edition of the Marineworld Revue, as they did in 1967. It was titled "Neptune's Noel" and included costumes for the trainers.

By March of 1968, scuba-outfitted, bikini-clad mermaids were performing the beginning of the Marineworld Revue by swimming with one of the porpoises, feeding him, and passing by the glass windows of the show stadium. The sea lions also joined the show during the act called "Porpoise Elementary School."

The 1968 Christmas show included Heidi the sea lion, Nemo the pilot whale, penguins, and of course porpoises. Built around the theme of different Christmas customs and celebrations, the animals were seen preparing to showcase their show "Christmas Around the World." But Nemo didn't feel well, and Dr. Blubber had to examine him. The doctor decided that Nemo had a broken heart because Mamuk the killer whale had taken his home, and the other animals hadn't given him a part in the special Christmas show. The porpoises, sea lions, and penguins took the audience to over twenty different countries, and in the end, Nemo was included, and his broken heart was mended.

By 1970 the penguins, going down a slide, had become a permanent part of the show, and whales had been added along with a new script for the Marineworld Revue. All of the animals had their own carefully choreographed and costumed acts set to music.

The 1974–1977 porpoise show was still called the Marineworld Revue, with porpoises leaping over hurdles, jumping through flaming hoops, playing math games, going to school, racing each other, and playing baseball—including having an argument with the umpire.

In 1978 the park began to refer to the animals as dolphins rather than porpoises. By 1979 the dolphin show was renamed the Disco Dolphin Revue.

Sea-Arama's dolphin stage got a redesign around 1980 or 1981, carrying a contemporary look of color coordinated graphic stripes. The show stadium had a Texas theme and the show was retitled A Salute to Texas, featuring dolphins performing high-flying pinwheels, quadruple jumps, tail walks, and more.

During the summer of 1986 there were three daily shows for dolphins with two alternating dolphin shows: The Sights and Sounds of Galveston, and Dolphin Dimensions.

The year 1989 saw Sea-Arama's best dolphin show: Dolphins: Myths and Legends. It was a two-part show with the first part being a typical announcer-led show with trainers outside of the water having the dolphins do various behaviors. But the magic began in the second half of the show, when the trainer jumped into the water with the dolphins. The announcer would stop talking and the beautiful music would begin. Together the dolphins and trainers would dance, leap, and race around the tank. As a finale, two dolphins would push the trainer by the feet down to the bottom of the pool before racing to the top and propelling the trainer high into the air. It was wonderful to watch and even better to experience if you were a trainer. The trainer would get out of the water and, just when you thought it couldn't get any better, the song "Walkin' on Sunshine" would begin, and the show would end with all five of the dolphins performing their best jumps and spins, one after another without stopping. There was no other park doing such an amazing dolphin show, and it always left everyone involved feeling like they had just participated in something very special.

# Backdrop and Stage

The stage and backdrop of the main porpoise show stadium changed quite a bit over the years. In the beginning, the early 1,000-seat stadium had a simple backdrop with one large show pool and four smaller holding tanks. There were no beaching platforms or walls to hide the holding pools.

In 1968 the backdrop was painted to show an elementary school scene with signs reading "Doctor" and "Coach" on fake doors, as well as a sign that read "Dolphin High" on the left. A red school house was in the middle and a large Sea-Arama logo was on the right. To the extreme right were clouds.

In 1969 the stage and backdrop received a major change as more walls and backdrops were added to separate the audience from the back of the stage. No longer could the audience see the porpoise and whale holding tanks backstage. Also, around 1969 or 1970 a slide was added to the right side of the stage for the penguins. A door was next to the slide with signs that read "Playground" and "Third Base."

By 1971 the backdrop had two medium-sized Sea-Arama logos with a red schoolhouse on the left and a penguin slide on the right. In addition, there was a tan bamboo building in the center of the stage backdrop and palm trees painted on the left.

The 1972 backdrop had two large Sea-Arama logos, with a red schoolhouse on the left, red shutters in the middle, and a slide on the right. Also, there was a landscape scene on the left with trees.

By June 1972 the backdrop had at least five painted palm trees over the left door, with a very large yellow flower to the very far left of the whale flume. In the middle were the red horizontal boards, with "Maison Rouge" on the top of the middle door. There was a big round Sea-Arama emblem to its right.

By July of 1972 the porpoise backdrop showed a cabin over the left door, with a ship to its left and a palm tree to its right.

The 1973 backdrop had two large Sea-Arama logos with a red schoolhouse on left and red shutters in the middle and a slide on the right. Also shown were a pier, water, beach, houses on the right, a red schoolhouse in the middle, two large Sea-Arama logos, palm trees on the left, and a river.

Sometime around 1975, the stage got a major overhaul when the sea lion stage was put in. This steel stage could be raised and lowered depending on the show.

The 1976 backdrop was yellow with two large Sea-Arama logos.

The 1978 backdrop was a jungle scene.

The 1982 backdrop was light blue with dark blue and yellow stripes and the words "Marineworld Revue." There was one Sea-Arama logo, and the words "Third Base" were painted on the wall.

The 1984 back drop was white, blue, and green with the state of Texas on the left side.

The 1985 backdrop was yellow with two ship wheels and a red stripe.

The 1986 backdrop was yellow with ship wheels and a green or blue stripe.

The 1987 backdrop was yellow with ship wheels and a red stripe.

The 1988-1990 backdrop was painted light and dark blue with a white wave and the Sea-Arama emblem.

Mermaid feeding Lafitte. *An All Tom Corp. postcard, author's collection.*

Lafitte, the Porpoise gets snack from Mermaid

Lafitte and Jim Parker during the porpoise show. *Courtesy of Susan and Ricky Lummus/Lemieux.*

Playing baseball in the porpoise show. *Courtesy of Greg May.*

Jumping for fish during the porpoise show.
*An All Tom Corp. postcard, author's collection.*

Jim Parker and Trace the porpoise.
*Courtesy of James P. Kelly Jr.*

Judy Zaun with porpoise. *Courtesy of Judy Zaun.*

Patty & Corky, two star Porpoises, take the hoops in stride

Patty and Corky hoop jump. *An All Tom Corp. postcard, author's collection.*

Fish jump with Judy Zaun.
*Courtesy of Judy Zaun.*

Squeaky does his world famous double flip.
*Courtesy of Linda Bwgen.*

*The Performing Porpoise Revue*
Porpoise show. *Author's collection.*

*Leap Through Fire Hoop*
Fire hoop leap at the porpoise show. *Author's collection.*

# Porpoise
# Petting/Feeding Pool
## 1970–1977?

One of the real crowd pleasers at Galveston's Sea-Arama Marineworld was the porpoise petting area, where visitors got to feed and pet porpoises similar to the ones they saw performing in the Marineworld Revue.

Originally the plan was to construct a pool on the east side of the park for six porpoises. It would be kidney shaped, hold 30,000 gallons of sea water, and be 40 feet long, 20 feet wide, and 10 feet deep. There is even a newspaper photograph of construction being started on that side of the park in May 1968. But ultimately the sea lion area that was used in 1968 by Jocko and Peaches was later converted to the porpoise petting pool.

The petting pool opened in 1970, but there were problems with the pool because the water depth was too low and too unstable for winter conditions. The result was the unfortunate loss of some porpoises one cold winter.

1970 porpoise petting pool. *Courtesy of Greg May.*

# Puppet Show
## 1977

In 1977 Sea-Arama presented a puppet show on the deck of the schooner *Southwind*. This show was a solo human act without an announcer. Besides puppets, the performer did sleight-of-hand tricks and told jokes. Between the various shows at the park, he would walk around with the puppets and entertain the visitors.

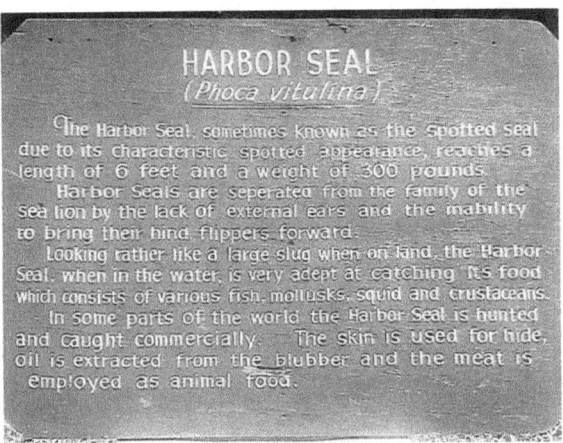

# Sea Lions and Seals

### Sea Lion and Seal Tank (Original location west of entrance)
July 1966–Mar 1969

### Sea Lion Feeding, Exhibit, Show (Round, rocky, four viewing areas, with shows only done during the summer)
May 1968–

### Harbor Seal Sea Lion Feeding Show (East of entrance)
June 1970–1990

### Seal Lions as part of Porpoise Show
Apr 1967–1972

### Sea Lions as part of Noah's Ark
1972–1976

### Elephant Seals in Noah's Ark (Fat Albert and Poncho)
1972–1976?

### Sea Lion Show (By themselves)
1975–1990

Sea-Arama acquired sea lions Heidi and Jocko soon after opening. In July 1966 the original sea lion tank exhibit was located west of the main building.

Sea lions were introduced into the porpoise show at the beginning of 1967. According to the trainers of this era, the sea lions performed in their own show immediately before or after the porpoise show, but it was billed and advertised as one show. Some of the tricks they did included jumping over a hurdle and through a hoop and clapping. Later in the show's history, the sea lions joined the porpoises in going to "Porpoise Elementary School."

The first seals didn't arrive until June 1968. At least one harbor seal was in the Oceanarium during the 1970s and frolicked with the mermaids in their show.

The original west side location of the sea lion tank was later converted into a seal feeding and summer show location. The seals were trained to do different tricks for food, and the public could also feed them.

Later, a new sea lion area was built on the west side and, by February 1970, this unusually designed exhibit and show enabled guests to view the playful animals from four levels: three underwater porthole viewing levels and one top deck viewing level. The display was 29 feet long, 17 feet wide, and 10 feet deep and had its own self-contained filtering system for water clarity. It was home to various sea lions, including 500-pound Jocko, Samantha, and Peaches. Guests were allowed to feed the sea lions and during the summer months there was a sea lion feeding show. This exhibit would later be turned into the porpoise petting pool.

There was another seal and sea lion feeding pool area east of the Oceanarium starting in 1971. Here, a wooden Polynesian bridge crossed the pond and allowed visitors to feed the seals and sea lions below. Fat Albert and (later) Poncho, the elephant seals, were also kept in this pool while they were at Sea-Arama.

Sea-Arama would sometimes send trainers and animals, including harbor seals, to local malls; this can be seen in one of the photos.

The Noah's Ark show also included sea lions. Heidi was one of the sea lions that performed in the Noah's Ark show, in addition to the elephant seal that was the star of this show. Eventually the sea lions got their own show in 1975 in the porpoise stadium, and this timeframe was regarded by many as having the best sea lion shows that Sea-Arama ever did. In the 1980s the sea lions were doing shows like "Sea Lion Water Olympics," "As the Marineworld Turns," "All My Sea Lions," and "The Case of the Missing Sea Lion." The comic antics of Sea-Arama's sea lions entertained audiences with their front flipper walks, high bows, and precision balancing—just a few examples of what they did. They would continue to have their own show until the park closed.

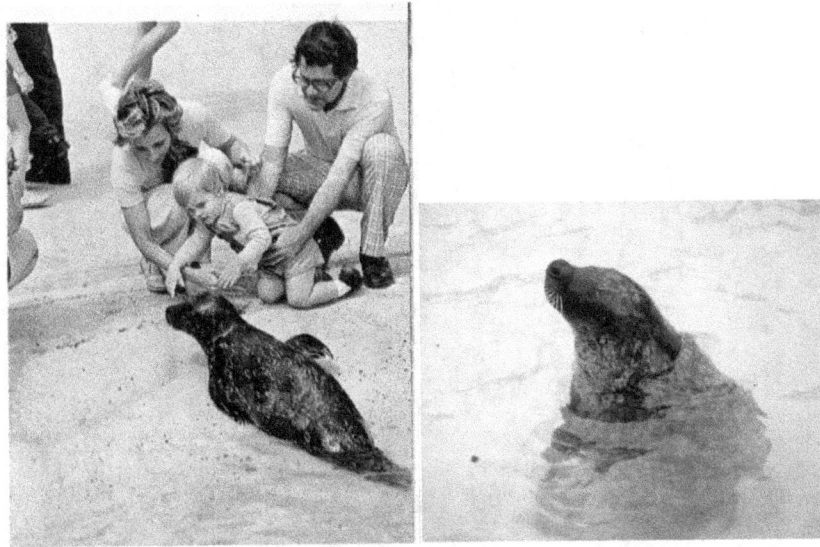

Seals. *Author's collection and Courtesy of John Masters.*

Heidi, The Sea Lion

*An All Tom Corp. postcard, author's collection.*

Sea lion show. *Courtesy of Greg May.*

Sea lion show. *Courtesy of Greg May.*

Jones kissing audience volunteer Janet Giusti Elledge in 1981. *Courtesy of Debra Giusti Morgan.*

One flipper stand in sea lion show. *Courtesy of Greg May.*

Sea lion feeding exhibit for Jocko and Peaches in '68. This exhibit would later become the porpoise petting pool. *Courtesy of Dale Ware Family Archives.*

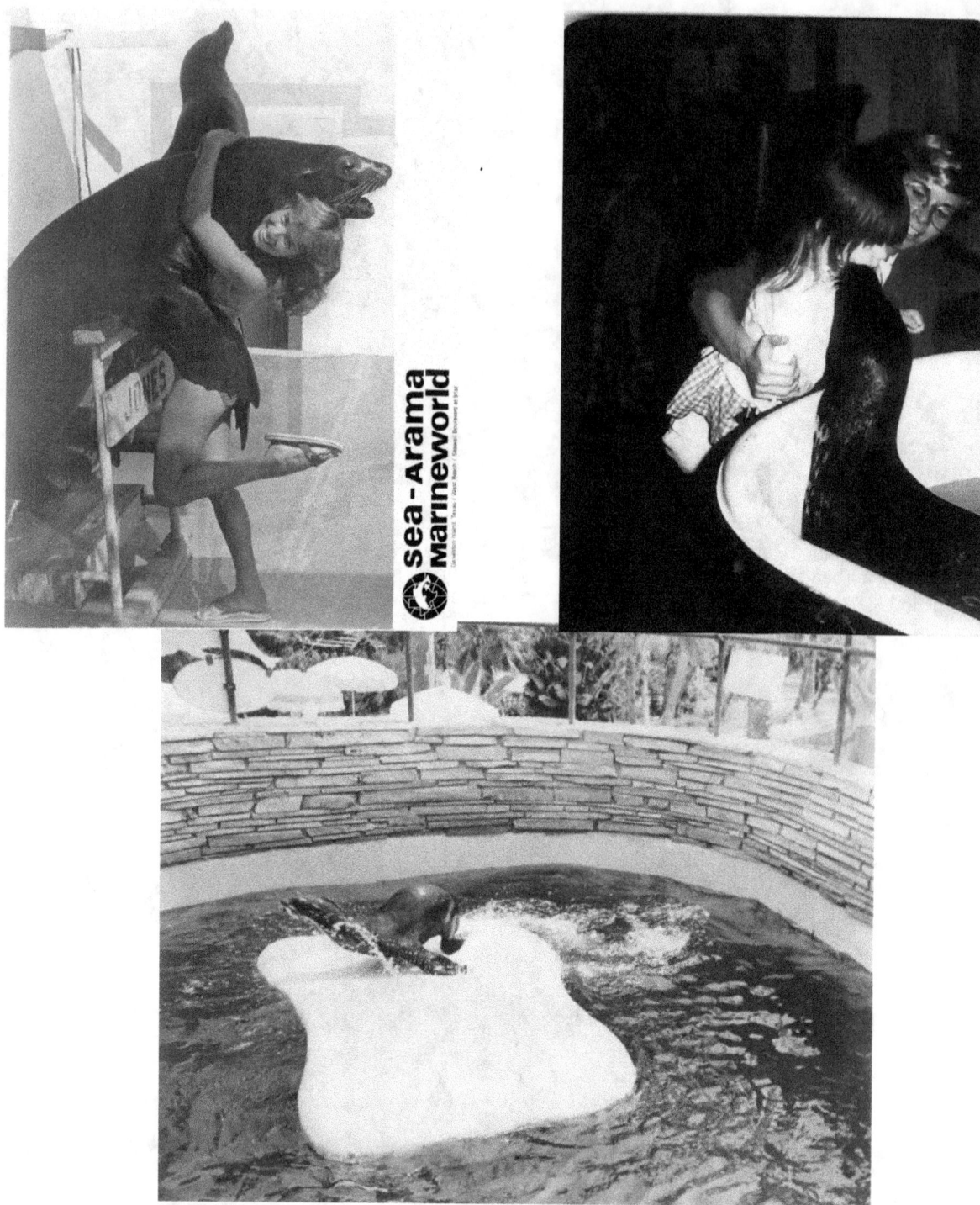

Top left: Jones and Debbie Marr. *Courtesy of Greg May.* Top right: Judy Zaun with Christmas Seal kid and Barnaby the harbor seal at a mall in Houston. *Courtesy of Judy Zaun.* Bottom: Peaches inside sea lion feeding exhibit. *Courtesy of Dale Ware Family Archives.*

# Ski Show
## April 1969–1989

The ski show was started in April of 1969 by John Humason (Doc Rail). It was performed on a four-acre man-made lake that had 150,000 square feet of water area. The 1500-seat ski stadium was the location for the ski show performed daily during the summer and on weekends immediately before and after the summer months. The ski show did not perform during the winter since the performers were all high-school and college students.

Doc Rail continued to direct the ski show until Terry Moore took it over in 1979. Terry remained at Sea-Arama until the last couple of years that Sea-Arama was open, when Ronnie Rouse was in charge of the ski show.

The ski show themes varied from year to year. The first was dubbed "The Pirates Lost Island Adventures." This first show used five boys and five girls and told the story of the pirate Jean Lafitte and his cohorts, shipwrecked on an island inhabited by beautiful mermaids. Lafitte actually did headquarter on Galveston Island, and his original campsite was near Sea-Arama.

Some of the themes used included:

- Pirates Lost Island Adventures (1969)
- Circus Theme "Greatest Show on Water" (1970, 1971)
- Wild Wet West (1972)
- S.M.A.S.H. (1973) First year of this show
- The Other America (1976)
- S.M.A.S.H (1977)
- My Favorite Fishing Hole (?)
- Title Unknown–Surfing to the Sounds of the '60s (1982)

- S.M.A.S.H. (1983)

- Hillbilly (1989)

"The Wild Wet West" was a spoof of many favorite Western characters.

"S.M.A.S.H." was a military farewell tribute to the men and women of the 4077 M.A.S.H. unit. In each show the skiers would perform various stunts such as barefoot water skiing, jumps over the platform and over other skiers, and human pyramid formations.

By the 1980s the 30-minute ski show was performed four to six times daily during the summer.

Three skiers jump over one. *Courtesy of Krystal Knutson.*

Bill Ansell, Terry Moore, Greg Scofelia. *An Astrocard Company postcard, author's collection.*

Bill Ansell without skis. *Courtesy of Greg May.*

Craig Janek and Greg Scofelia without skis. *Courtesy of Gin Thom.*

Steve Harris, Mark Johnson, Jack Hammit underneath circa 1970. *Courtesy of Greg May.*

Kim Piel Conner on top, Linda Meyer Sivy, Julie Brown, Danny Scheffler, Nick O'Donohoe, Darrell Charles. *Courtesy of Greg May.*

# Snakes

### Snake Show (added to Alligator Show)
### Apr 1970–1976

### Snake Display
### June 1970–1975 to ?

### Snake/Reptile Show (no Alligators)
### 1977–May 1985

The Snake Show, added in 1970, was the newest addition to the Alligator Show. It originally involved the handling of three snakes: A South American 14-foot boa constrictor, an American diamondback rattlesnake, and a cobra.

The diamondback carried enough venom to kill a grown man in about three hours. Sea-Arama handlers demonstrated the quick-striking ability of the diamondback by allowing it to strike at their hands and legs. Most of the time they were quick enough to avoid the bite, but newspaper articles tell the story of a number of Sea-Arama handlers who had to go to the hospital.

The performance most talked about and remembered involved the deadly cobras. In the early days of Sea-Arama, the park used king cobras. These snakes were venom spitters, and their venom was so poisonous that if venom touched the skin, the person could suffer severe nerve damage. The park later changed to using monocled cobras from Southeast Asia. These snakes didn't spit, and their venom was less poisonous—even though they were billed by the park as the most poisonous snakes in the world. The Sea-Arama snake handlers charmed these creatures with their bare hands, and in later years, the finale of the show would be the trainer placing the "Kiss of Death" on the top of the Buddha cobra's head.

One interesting note is that in the 1970s the trainers would move the snake show into the Oceanarium during the winter months because it would be too cold outside for the reptiles to perform.

Soon after the snake show started, the park created a snake display for the public. It included boas, rattlesnakes, cobras, and non-poisonous snakes in their natural settings, with signs explaining interesting facts about the reptiles.

In 1977 the alligator show was dropped; from then on, the show was referred to as either the snake show or reptile show. Also, in 1977, Robin Rader handled snakes and was the only female snake handler in the country at the time.

By the end of the snake show era in the 1980s, the advertising referred to Sea-Arama's snake oil salesman, Slippery Sam. He would perform his reptile show alongside his rustic old "snake coach" and would work with deadly Texas diamondback rattlers, Burmese pythons, and a snap-happy gator.

Ken Jones. *Courtesy of Dale Ware Family Archives.*

Bob Putgnat kissing the cobra in the snake show in the late 1970s or early 1980s. *Courtesy of Tim Cromie.*

Bob Putgnat and Stella Musick Jares in the snake show. *Courtesy of Tim Cromie.*

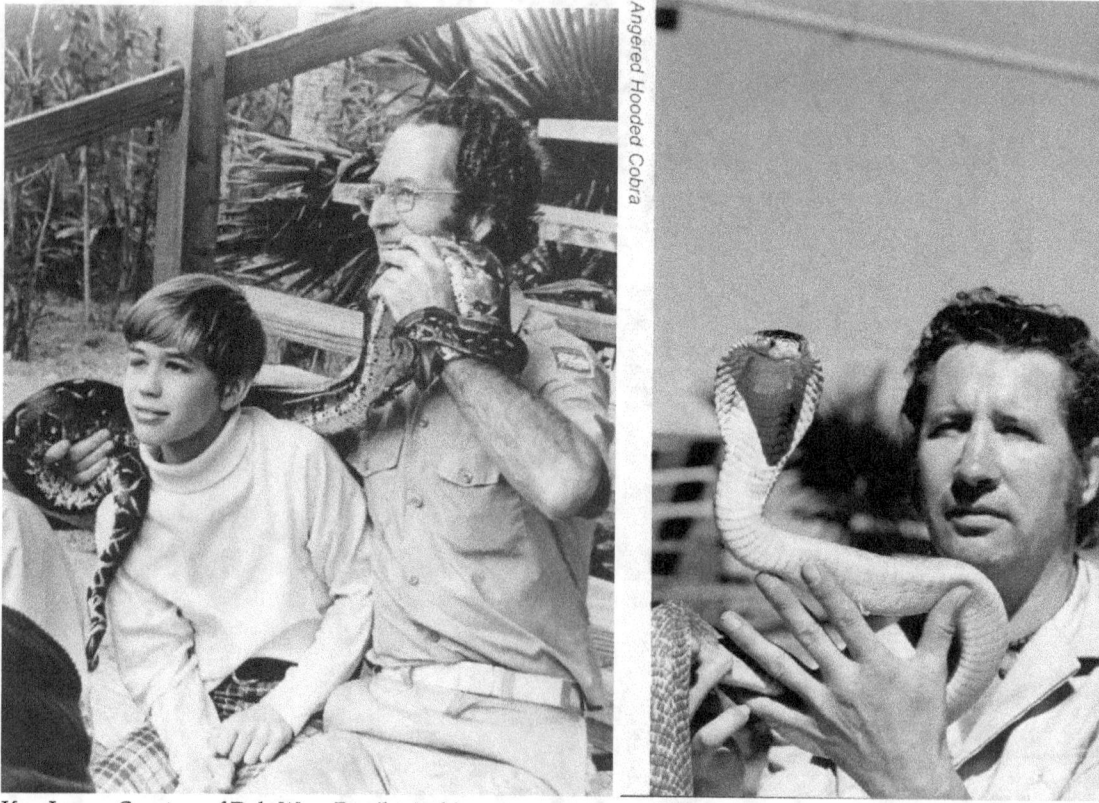

Angered Hooded Cobra

Ken Jones. *Courtesy of Dale Ware Family Archives.*

Gene Ogle with cobra. *Author's collection.*

Kiss of Death

Gene Ogle performing the "Kiss of Death." *Author's collection.*

# *Southwind* Schooner
## Feb 1972–1979 to ?

## Musical Variety Show (on the deck)
### June 1976–Sept 1977

One of the few static displays at Sea-Arama was the 103-foot schooner *Southwind*. Commissioned the *Sartartia* in Boothbay, Maine, in 1929 by Houstonian Benjamin Clayton, *Southwind* was a two-masted wooden ship with a beam of 22 feet and a main mast that rose 92 feet from the deck.

Over the years she had some famous Hollywood skippers, such as Charles "Chuck" Jones, Joseph Maniewicz, George Brent, Jack Warner, and Jackie Coogan. When Warner was the owner, he let Errol Flynn take the schooner out on trips.

*Southwind* was as extravagant as she was sleek. Two guest staterooms with two bunks each were separated by the guest bath. The owner's stateroom had a private bath. A completely stocked galley was on board, as well as captain's quarters and forward crew quarters and another bathroom.

She returned to the Houston-Galveston area in the 1960s when she was purchased by D. F. W. Downey for an estimated $100,000.

In September of 1971, John Humason, also known as "Doc Rail" of Nassau Bay, Texas, purchased *Southwind*. She had been berthed at Morgan's Point, Texas, for a number of years and was badly in need of repair. Doc Rail was refitting her at the Galveston Yacht Basin when a freak storm blew out of the northeast on November 23, 1971, with winds up to 30 knots. *Southwind* beat herself to death and sank in 35 feet of water. She had taken a 4' X 4' hole in her starboard side at the beam. Her keel had also pulled away from the bottom.

She stayed at the bottom of the basin for about a week and a half until salvaged and towed to the shipyards. At that time, Ed Moore, Executive V.P. of Sea-Arama, negotiated a settlement to acquire the sailing yacht. Sea-Arama officials had *Southwind* raised and the gash in her stern patched. Through the help of a mobile crane, she was raised on a submersible barge and towed to Kelso Marine.

In 1972 *Southwind* came to Sea-Arama, where she was refurbished. Plans were made for her interior to be re-outfitted in 1973 and 1974 and for her to be established as a floating museum. In the end, just her top deck and portions of her hull were displayed for several years at the park attraction.

A marriage was performed on her deck on September 29, 1973, by group sales secretary Fran Lloyd and her fiancé, Fred Galbreath. The wedding party was dressed in nautical red, white, and blue.

By June of 1973, Sea-Arama was advertising *Southwind* as a new attraction, along with a Bangladesh sampan that was listed on the 1973 and 1974 maps. Also, in the 1970s Sea-Arama provided a recorded narration about *Southwind* as the public viewed the ship.

In 1976 and 1977 Sea-Arama had its first and only song-and-dance musical variety show, which debuted on *Southwind's* deck. The song and dance musical was performed entirely by high school and college students from the Galveston area. Performances were offered four times daily. Songs included "Bali Hai," "Calypso," "Red Sails in the Sunset," and "The Good Ship Lollipop."

In February of 1979, toward the end of its life, Sea-Arama announced in the *Galveston Daily* newspaper that it had "plans to isolate *Southwind* and create an atmosphere by narration and musical background that would allow visitors to relax and envision the romantic days of the schooner." Unfortunately, after years of being abused by hurricanes and tropical storms, *Southwind* finally succumbed to the ravages of termites. She was dismantled and partially salvaged, with her binnacle being donated to the Weems Maritime collection.

The author of this book contacted a former *Southwind* crew member, Hollis Danvers, and was granted permission to include this additional bit of her history:

*Southwind was purchased either in late 1963 or early 1964 by Doyle Downey of Houston. He bought the boat in Newport Beach. He sent the boat through the Panama Canal to Galveston. I found them there in early May 1964. They were in the Galveston Shrimp Basin, across the jetty from the Galveston Yacht Club, which was too shallow for them. A new captain had just opened Southwind and was taking on crew. I hired on as deckhand at age 24. After two weeks, we took Southwind on a shakedown and publicity cruise to Aransas Pass, TX, where Southwind was photographed for the cover of the weekly magazine supplement of the Houston Chronicle. Next, we motored to Miami, and then on to New York. Southwind had carpentry and electronics upgrades at Minneford*

*Boat Yard, in City Island. In August we sailed to Newport and joined the spectator fleet for the America's Cup Races. Hurricane Gladys closed all middle Atlantic ports for a week or so. After that, we sailed to Hamilton, Bermuda, and on to St. Thomas, USVI, and English Harbor, Antigua, where we joined the Nicholson charter fleet for the eastern Caribbean. During the winter of 1964 we sailed to St. Maarten, St. Barthelemy, Guadaloupe, Martinique, St. Lucia, St. Vincent, the Grenadines, Barbados, and Grenada. In Barbados we were hauled and bottom-cleaned in the British dry-dock built in 1893. Then we sailed back up the Grenadines to Tobago Keys (St. Vincent). We had Christmas Day and New Year's Day in Bequia. I left Southwind New Year's Eve 1964. I saw the boat one more time, sometime in the 1970s, again in Galveston. She had become a walk-on tourist attraction up on blocks at Galveston's Sea-Arama. I have just finished a short story about my time aboard Southwind. It is called "The Glass Factory," which is available for purchase on Amazon.*

Southwind before coming to Sea-Arama. *Courtesy of Hollis Danvers.*

Southwind before Sea-Arama. *Courtesy of Carol Glazerman and Hollis Danvers*

# Three Bears Show
## Feb 1976–Oct 1977

Sea-Arama acquired bears around June 1975 from Sea Life Park in Texas. By the time the show started in the first quarter of 1976, there were four bears. Sea-Arama then advertised the training sessions that the public could observe, which were based on positive reinforcement. The park was proud of the fact that they didn't remove teeth or claws or muzzle the bears for training or shows. The bears were learning how to play basketball, walk upright on a drum, dance, roll over, tuck themselves into bed, slide, and seesaw with a friend.

When they arrived, they were two years old and weighed 250 lbs. It was anticipated that they would grow to six feet and weigh 500 lbs.

In their two years at the park, Sea-Arama advertised the bears performing in "Goldilocks and the Three Bears" and as "dancing bears."

Three Bears show.
*Author's collection.*

Your family will be amazed by Sea-Arama's unique Three Bears act.

Judy Zaun on left during the Three Bears show. *Courtesy of Judy Zaun.*

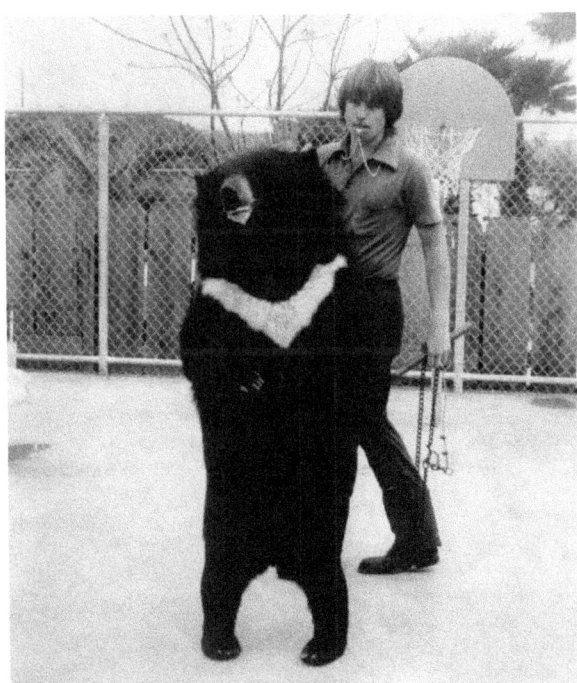

Dave Richtman with bear. *Courtesy of Greg May.*

Judy Zaun with bear. *Courtesy of Judy Zaun.*

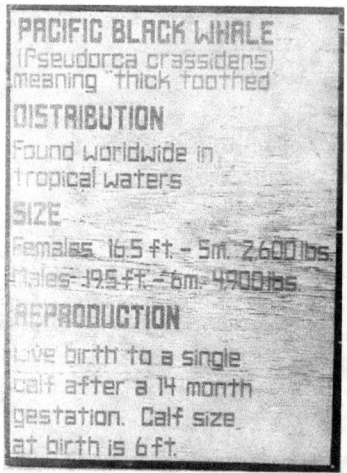

PACIFIC BLACK WHALE
(Pseudorca crassidens)
meaning "thick toothed"
DISTRIBUTION
Found worldwide in
tropical waters
SIZE
Females 16.5 ft - 5m. 2,600 lbs.
Males 19.5 ft - 6m. 4,900 lbs.
REPRODUCTION
Live birth to a single
calf after a 14 month
gestation. Calf size
at birth is 6 ft.

# Whales
## June 1968–1990

**Nemo (Pilot Whale)**
June 1968–Apr 30, 1970

**Mamuk (Killer Whale)**
Oct 29, 1968–June 14, 1974

**Nooka (Killer Whale)**
Aug 20, 1970–Mar 18, 1971

**Tiffany (Pilot Whale)**
May 1975–June 13, 1975

**Nami (Pacific Black Whale)**
Apr 2, 1989–May 3, 1989

**Tanoshi (Pacific Black Whale)**
Apr 2, 1989–Aug 1990

The whales were the stars of the show at Sea-Arama. Over the years the park had six whales that performed in the Pilot Whale Show, the Killer Whale Show, and the Marineworld Revue. Nemo, the first whale, had been orphaned before coming to Sea-Arama. When he arrived, he had to be fed 40 pounds of whipped cream a day. He came from San Diego's SeaWorld and brought his toys with him—a tractor tire and a fire hose. His part of the Marineworld Revue in 1969 included going through the routine of a kid on his first day at school, doing the high jump, retrieving objects, being examined by a doctor, and playing baseball.

Mamuk, king of the Sea-Arama whales, arrived in October 1968. The 13-foot, 2,300-pound killer whale was purchased from Don Goldsberry of the Seattle Marine Aquarium for $40,000. At that time Sea-Arama was one of a very few attractions in the world to have a killer whale. To prepare for his arrival, Sea-Arama built a 13-foot-deep, 50-foot-long holding pen that held 80,000 gallons of water and cost $66,000. Thirty thousand pounds of reinforcing steel were used in the construction, and the filtering system was tied into the existing system.

When Mamuk arrived, he was a little over two years old and ate 1,300 fish daily. The park anticipated he would grow to 13,000 pounds, eating 3,000 fish a day.

The killer whale training sessions became part of the Marineworld Revue until, in July of 1969, Mamuk finally had his own show. By 1971, Mamuk was presenting his version of a Texas-style rodeo called "The Last Round-Up." It included spectacular jumps and ended with a splash that sprayed the first four rows.

While Mamuk was at Sea-Arama, the park also purchased another killer whale: Lil Nooka, also known as Nooka. He was purchased from Seattle and moved to Sea-Arama in 1970. Lil Nooka was chosen from the captured whales because it was hoped his young age would make him easier to train and keep healthy. The staff hoped that Lil Nooka and Mamuk would begin performing together by spring of 1971. However, after only seven months at Sea-Arama, Lil Nooka died of asphyxiation.

Mamuk continued his reign at Sea-Arama until June of 1974, when he too passed away. After Mamuk died, another pilot whale was flown in from California, but Tiffany the pilot whale only lasted about one month.

The park went many years without a whale until 1989, when they purchased two Pacific black whales, or false killer whales as they are also known. They were the park's last hope to turn things around. When the first one died very quickly, the end of the park was just around the corner. Tanoshi, the second whale, remained at Sea-Arama until after the park sold. Eventually she was sold as well as the other animals.

Nemo the Flying Whale Says "No" to a Shot

Howard Picard with Nemo. *An All Tom Corp. postcard, author's collection.*

Nemo the pilot whale with unknown group. *Courtesy of Dale Ware Family Archives.*

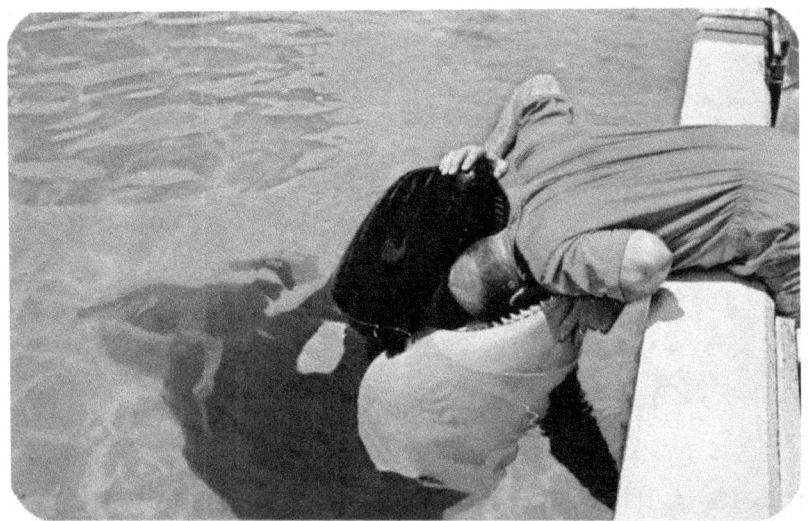

A Look into the Mouth of Mamuk The Killer Whale

Special Show of Mamuk, The Killer Whale

Mermaid riding Mamuk, a 3000 Lb. Killer Whale

Top: Howard Picard and Mamuk. *An All Tom Corp. postcard, author's collection.* Left: Mamuk performing. *An All Tom Corp.postcard, author's collection.* Right: Melissa McClellan with Mamuk, ca. 1969–1972. *An All Tom Corp. postcard, author's collection.*

# Other Places in the Park

**Tropical Gardens** (self-guided walk through foliage and landscaping)
July 1966–Aug 1968

**Tropical Gardens** (lagoon, waterfall, picnic area, exotic birds, Octopus Grotto, sea lion exhibit/feeding show arena, porpoise petting pool)
Aug 1968–1975 to ?

**Pirates Nook**
Oct 1968–1984 to ?

**Pink Porpoise Ice Cream Parlor**
Oct 1968–1973?

**Oleander Garden**
Mar 1969–1983?

**Treasure Chest Gift Shop**
1965–1990

**Camera Shop/Shutter Shop**
1965–1968 to ?

**Garden of the Gods** (two hand-carved tikis, dining tables surround the garden patio, Tiki Hut snack bar)
Feb 1970–1976 to ?

In addition to the sea life on exhibit, Sea-Arama offered beautiful tropical gardens, a restaurant and snack bars, and gift and camera shops.

The Treasure Chest Gift Shop was a permanent fixture throughout the park's life, even though the look of it changed over the years. It offered beautiful and unusual gift items and is mentioned in detail in one of the stories in the chapter "Sea-Arama Marineworld Stories."

The camera shop also varied its looks and offered black and white or color film, flash bulbs, and other equipment throughout its years of existence.

The Pirates Nook Restaurant was close to the front entrance, with glassed–in seating and an outdoor patio for viewing of the Tropical Gardens and waterfall and exotic birds. Sea-Arama's upstairs Crow's Nest dining area offered an elevated view of the Tropical Gardens.

A further addition to Sea-Arama's food facilities was the Pink Porpoise Ice Cream Parlor, where various flavors of ice cream and malts were served as well as cotton candy.

In the mid-1970s there was also the Seahorse snack bar upstairs, the Whale Bar snacks, and the Tiki Pavilion, among others.

At the same time the ski show started in 1969, the park divided some of the existing lakes into smaller lakes by creating two levees, constructed with special locks to provide adequate water circulation. This can be seen in one of the photos.

The year 1969 was also when the Alligator Island and swamp were built. A 7,500-foot island was constructed with divided pools to accommodate 20 alligators and a 600-seat covered stadium. The park then created a swamp with walk bridges and moss-draped trees.

A year later, a special Jean Lafitte's Pirate Raft Ride took guests across to the island. This was the first ride at Sea-Arama and involved two pirate-style barges, each holding approximately 40 to 50 people. The ride began at the seal and sea lion feeding area and traveled across the water-ski area to the alligator and snake show area. But as attendance increased, this ride was eliminated in favor of a permanent walkway.

In 1970 the park added two hand-carved South Sea Islands tikis and completed the Polynesian design that was begun the year before.

Sea-Arama was known for its lush tropical gardens and paths leading through the foliage. By 1972 there was a Palm Tree Walk that included windmill, thatch, whiskey, toddy, jelly, Chinese fountain, aristocrat, Washingtonia, Mediterranean, European fan, and queen palms. The golden dew drop shrubs were grown from seed, and the candle trees had re-seeded themselves. Other plants included Jerusalem cherry, confederate rose, soft yucca, cape honeysuckle, pony tail palm, plumbago, century plants, rubber trees, shower of gold, pittosporum, Burma honeysuckle, bottle brush, and day lilies. The park was especially proud of the Vitex trifolia (Arabian lilac), a native of Malesia.

In addition to all of this flora, the park had an Oleander Garden that was started by the National Oleander Society.

On July 4, 1978, a ribbon cutting ceremony was held to open the Aqua Thrill Way. In charge of the ceremonies were Sea-Arama Marineworld's general manager, Dale Ware, Mayor John Unbehagen, and Aquatractions Inc. vice president Robert E. Howie. This water toboggan slide was now open to the general public and was operated by Sea-Arama Marineworld. It was located on park property at 9028 Seawall Blvd. Billed as a "slide on the wild side,'" the attraction was designed after the Alpine toboggan runs in Switzerland. The slides were called "flumes," and Aqua Thrill Way had three 450-foot flumes. Change rooms were available and refreshments were also offered. Guests could ride any one or all three flumes as many times as possible in a 30-minute period. Sea-Arama was excited about it because at the time, they had plans for developing an amusement center in that area, and the toboggan slide was the first part of their expansion plans. However, the amusement center did not become a reality.

Over the years the park had many themes. There was a Caribbean theme, Bicentennial theme, South Sea Islands theme—and Sea-Arama even created snow one year for a Christmas special.

Goodwill ambassadors in costume were popular at Sea-Arama and included Buttons the Dancing Dolphin and Tulip the Dancing Bear in 1976, and Salty the Seahorse and Ollie the Octopus in 1978. The costumes each cost $1,500 and they were extremely hot to wear. The person inside saw through the mouth of the character. The costumes were cleaned in the washing machines.

Like other parks, Sea-Arama had theme songs and jingles that many people still remember.

Song:
*Come see the sights,*
*Come see the show.*
*Come to Sea-Arama super*
*sea show by the sea shore!*

Jingle:
*Sea-Arama Marineworld,*
*On sunny Galveston isle,*
*Take your family down for fun,*
*In the semi-tropic sun,*
*And you may never want to go,*
*Never ever want to go home.*

Gift Shop items displayed at the 2012 Reunion. *Author's collection.*

Sea-Arama costumed character with Girl Scouts. *Courtesy of Krystal Knutson.*

Park Administration building when the park first opened. Located near where the bird show stadium would be. *Courtesy of James P. Kelly. Jr.*

Entrance to Sea-Arama in 1971. *Courtesy of Greg May.*

Tim Gould

Lagoon and waterfall area in 1973.
*Courtesy of Krystal Knutson.*

John Kerivan (left), Head Curator, in the lab.
*Courtesy of Krystal Knutson.*

Locks being constructed between lakes for new killer Whale stadium in 1969. *Courtesy of Krystal Knutson.*

# Sea-Arama Marineworld Publicity
## 1965–1990

The Sea-Arama publicity staff members were an important part of the park throughout its history. Relentlessly getting the word out to every Texas paper and many more across the world, the staff advertised new animals, new shows and exhibits, and even untimely deaths as they occurred. Sometimes plans that weren't yet finalized would be publicized to garner interest and attendance at the park.

Because of their work, Sea-Arama became a vital part of the community, and with their help the park hosted scouting events, choir and band competitions, and school field trips. Sea-Arama sponsored several events over the years, including a Halloween party in 1978 with local merchants offering prizes.

Girl Scouts and Campfire Girls were saluted every March, and Boy Scouts were saluted each weekend in February. Other groups that came to Sea-Arama included school field trips, high school senior trips, church youth groups, YMCA, YWCA, fraternal organizations, summer camps, daycare nurseries, senior citizens, bus tour groups, military, conventions, and company outings.

Mark Sweet as Willy Wonka in 1985. *Courtesy of Krystal Knutson.*

Sea-Arama shark bumper stickers. *Courtesy of Krystal Knutson.*

Melissa McClellan and Mamuk ca. 1969–1972. *Courtesy of Dale Ware Family Archives.*

Compaq advertising shoot with Greg Whittaker and Jim Dobberstine. *Courtesy of Jim Dobberstine.*

1986 McDonald's place mat. *Author's collection.*

1986 Family Membership Card. *Author's collection*

School program brochure. *Author's collection.*

# Marine Mammal Stranding Network
## 1983–1990

The Texas Marine Mammal Stranding Network began in 1980, and by 1983 Sea-Arama had been appointed as the rescue center for stranded and injured marine mammals. In 1986 Sea-Arama was expanding its educational program to include information on stranded and injured animals.

Sea-Arama's involvement in helping stranded animals was evident long before the Stranding Network formed. Sea-Arama's objective was always to not only save injured and stranded animals, but also to widen the public's knowledge and understanding of marine animals.

Over the years Sea–Arama acquired many animals unexpectedly. A rare 600-pound turtle became entangled in the trolling net of a shrimp boat and was brought to the park. Pilgrim the pygmy sperm whale was brought to the park in the 1970s. Children who caught strange creatures along the beach brought them to the biologists at Sea-Arama, who happily identified them for the future scientists.

In 1978 Lucky the dolphin was rescued by the Marine Mammal Stranding Network and brought to Sea-Arama. Odie the baby sperm whale was brought to Sea-Arama in 1989 and received much publicity and care. Even after the park closed, local conservationists were allowed to use vital resources at the park in their efforts to help animals that had been stranded or injured.

Unfortunately, many of the animals that were rescued and brought to Sea-Arama died, but in every situation the staff and curators of Sea-Arama made every effort to save the animal's life. Often the trainers, staff, and volunteers would be in the water with the animal for days at a time, holding it up so it could breathe and force feeding it in hopes it would live.

Newspapers reported that, as of July 1986, Lucky the dolphin was the only mammal that had survived a rescue from the Gulf of Mexico.

Pilgrim the pygmy sperm whale (coated in white zinc oxide), 1970s. *Author's collection.*

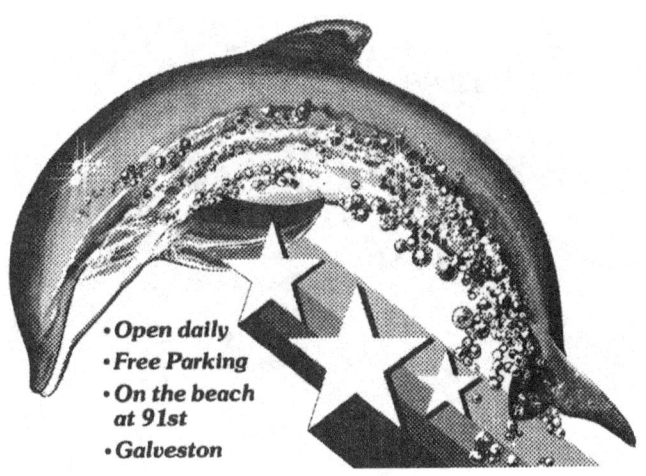

- Open daily
- Free Parking
- On the beach at 91st
- Galveston

# Sea-Arama Marineworld
# Through the Years

# 1965

Sea-Arama Marineworld publicized its opening date as April of 1965. On the week of March 11, 1965, Sea-Arama transferred its eight porpoises from temporary outdoor training tanks into the stadium tanks in the main show stadium in preparation for this opening date. As April approached, the opening date had to be postponed because of difficulties in installing a sea water intake line. The cause of this delay was windy weather in the Gulf of Mexico.

Animals and employees had been in training for months, some employees even going to Florida to be trained at other parks. Finally, on November 6, Sea-Arama held its News and Press Day at 2:00 p.m. The 1,000-seat stadium was two-thirds full, and those in attendance included Mayor Edward Schreiber of Galveston. The shows were well received, and Sea-Arama prepared for the next day—the day everyone had been anticipating.

On November 7 the park opened to the public for the first time. As already mentioned, the sheer number of visitors meant that additional porpoise shows were necessary. The public delighted in seeing the animals high-jumping, tandem pole jumping, putting out a fire, collecting and carrying hoops, "singing" in a trio, bowing to the audience, playing a baseball game with two trainers, passing a football, walking backward, and doing other tricks.

The Oceanarium offered underwater feedings by the divers and 28 individual jewel tanks for viewing of various native and exotic fish. Besides the sea life on exhibit, Sea-Arama offered a beautiful gift shop located on the ground level, managed by Mrs. Bell Fenton.

Another Sea-Arama service was the camera shop, which was located at the main entrance and managed by Miss Dottie Sampson, who later became a sea lion trainer at the park.

Porpoise Show November 6, 1965. *Courtesy of Remembering Sea-Arama website.*

Trainer Randy Orkish with porpoise. *Courtesy of James P. Kelly Jr.*

Trainer Denny Furchow with dolphin.
*Courtesy of James P. Kelly Jr.*

Diver in the Oceanarium. *Courtesy of James P. Kelly Jr.*

**Some of the employees:**
Ann Trent–Aquarist
B. Rex Shields–Vice president
Belle Fenton–Gift shop manager
Ben Green–Diver, announcer
Bill Veale–Collector, diver
Bob Landers–Pump man
Bob Rutledge–Director of construction and maintenance
Brooks Robins–Trainer
Clark Bowers–Head trainer
Dave McSpadden–Director of public relations
Denny Furchow–Trainer, diver
Denny O Ingram JR–Secretary of corporation
Dottie Samson–Trainer, camera shop manager
Esta May Bolden–Janitor, gardener
Fred Eckert–General manager
Glenda Foster Snipes–Office secretary
Henry Ramsey–Treasurer of corporation
Howard Picard–Diver
Hunter Miller–General manager until November '65
Jack Dismukes–Director of the corporation, board member

James (Jim) Bierman–Diver
James (Jim) Kelly, Jr.–Head curator
Jerry DeOrr–Head announcer and exhibit supervisor
Jim Beatty–Diver
Jim Parker–Trainer
John Simpson–Board member
J.W. Scarbrough JR–Board member
Lee Kane–General manager until March '65
Lucille Ray–Director of landscaping
Norris Brown–Landscaping
Orange Telford–Landscaping
Randy Orkisch–Trainer
Richard Klaerner–Board member, director
Steve Cowan–Master of ceremonies
Teeny Kelly–Trainer
Tom Crauson–Trainer
Tom Whitman–First aquarist at the park, assistant curator
Travis Larue–President
Willie Dennis–Gardener

**Some of the Animals:**
Patty–porpoise
Squeaky–porpoise
Lafitte–porpoise
Alvin (Al)–porpoise
Trace–porpoise
Black–porpoise
Sinbad–porpoise
Kiko–porpoise
Lucy–porpoise
Seahorses

Arapaima
Rays
Piranha
Triggerfish
Spiny lobster
Giant sea turtle
Green moray eel
280-lb. jewfish
27 varieties of freshwater Texas fish

# 1966

By January of 1966 Sea-Arama was already thinking of how to improve and expand the park. At this point there were no sea lions in the shows or on exhibit, but Heidi, the first sea lion at Sea-Arama, was being taught tricks by trainers Teeny Kelly, Kathryn McDonald, and others in preparation for inclusion into the porpoise show.

In June a new expanded schedule of shows began with the Oceanarium opening from 10:00 a.m. to 5:00 p.m. with shows at 11:00 a.m., 12:30 p.m., 2:00 p.m., 3:30 p.m., and 5:00 p.m.

By July, Sea-Arama had put a snack bar in the picnic area as well as more landscaping. This area would become known as the Tropical Gardens. Also, the towering palm trees along the west walkway to the main entrance were transplanted after having survived hurricane Carla in 1961. Some of the pieces of wood and shingles forced into the trees by tornado gusts could still be seen.

The park also added the first sea lion tank with two sea lions and acquired more by the end of July. At this time Sea-Arama consisted of the Oceanarium, five porpoise shows, four porpoise living pools, 28 jewel aquarium tanks, snack bar, sea lion tank, gift shop, restrooms, and five underwater feedings by divers.

In August, a porpoise trainer, with the help of a University of Texas surgeon, reached down into the porpoise's throat to retrieve 20 inches of rubber caulking he had swallowed. This procedure saved the porpoise's life.

By September Sea-Arama was getting closer to adding sea lions to the porpoise show, but curator Jim Kelly thought it would be the following spring or summer before they were ready. There were five sea lions in the sea lion display, and Heidi would be the one to perform in sea lion shows, since she had already learned a few tricks—jumping over a hurdle, jumping through a hoop, and clapping. At this time the trainers weren't able to spend a lot of time training the sea lions because they needed to focus on the porpoises, but they were hopeful they could get back to the sea lions later in 1966.

When winter arrived, trainer Kathy McDonald and others were busy training sea lions Jocko and Farouk. Her hope was to have these sea lions ready for a show by the beginning of summer 1967.

In November Sea-Arama curators were excited as they had acquired a northern pike fish from Canada and a rare red tail catfish from South America for the Oceanarium.

In December Sea-Arama installed three emersion tank heaters for the Oceanarium and porpoise tanks. During the previous winter about half of the fish, including the barracudas, had died and two of the porpoises had been near death due to the cold weather.

Heidi the sea lion and Teeny Kelly, January 1966. *Courtesy of Teeny Kelly.*

Heidi in January 1996. *Courtesy of Teeny Kelly.*

Kathryn McDonald and Farouk. *Courtesy of Kathryn (Kathy) McDonald Taubert & digitization, courtesy of Robert Cubbage.*

Kathryn McDonald and Farouk. *Courtesy of Kathryn (Kathy) McDonald Taubert & digitization, courtesy of Robert Cubbage.*

Clark Bowers. *A Mirro-Krome H.S. Crocker Co. postcard.*

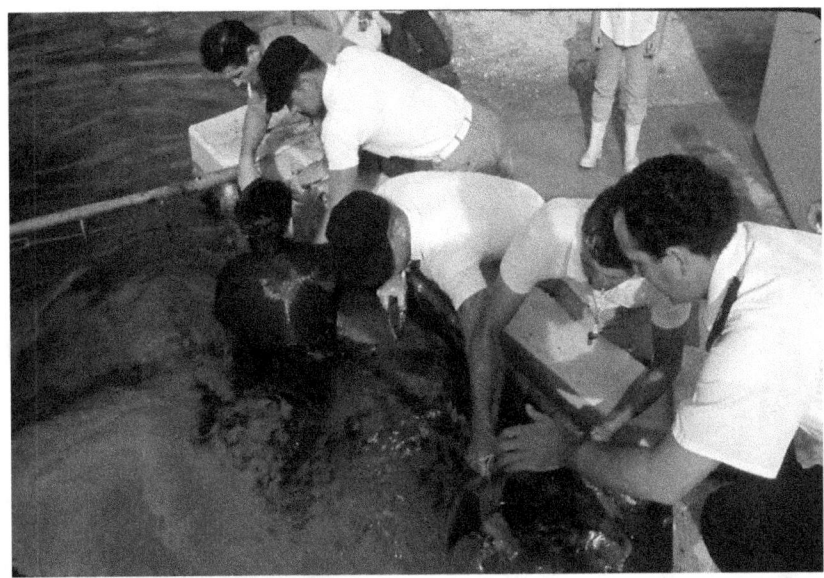

Removing Squeaky the porpoise to get the dowel rod he had swallowed. *Courtesy of Kathryn (Kathy) McDonald Taubert & digitization, courtesy of Robert Cubbage.*

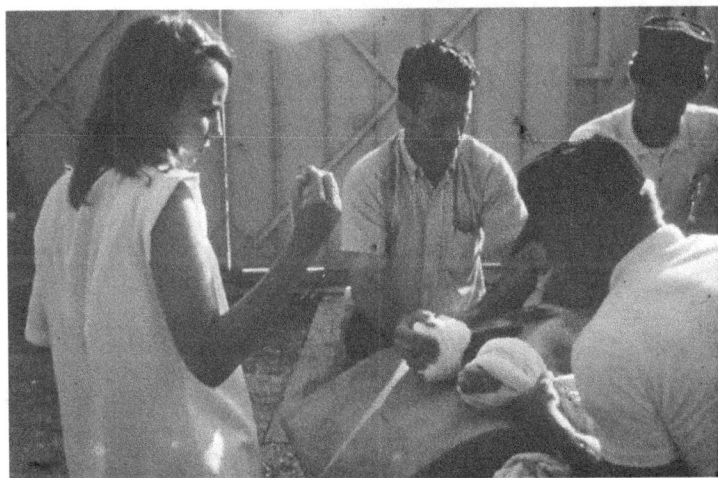

Kathryn McDonald preparing to reach into Squeaky's stomach to retrieve wooden dowel. (See Sea-Arama Marineworld Stories). *Courtesy of Kathryn (Kathy) McDonald Taubert & digitization, courtesy of Robert Cubbage.*

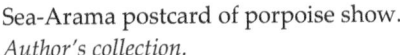

Sea-Arama postcard of porpoise show. *Author's collection.*

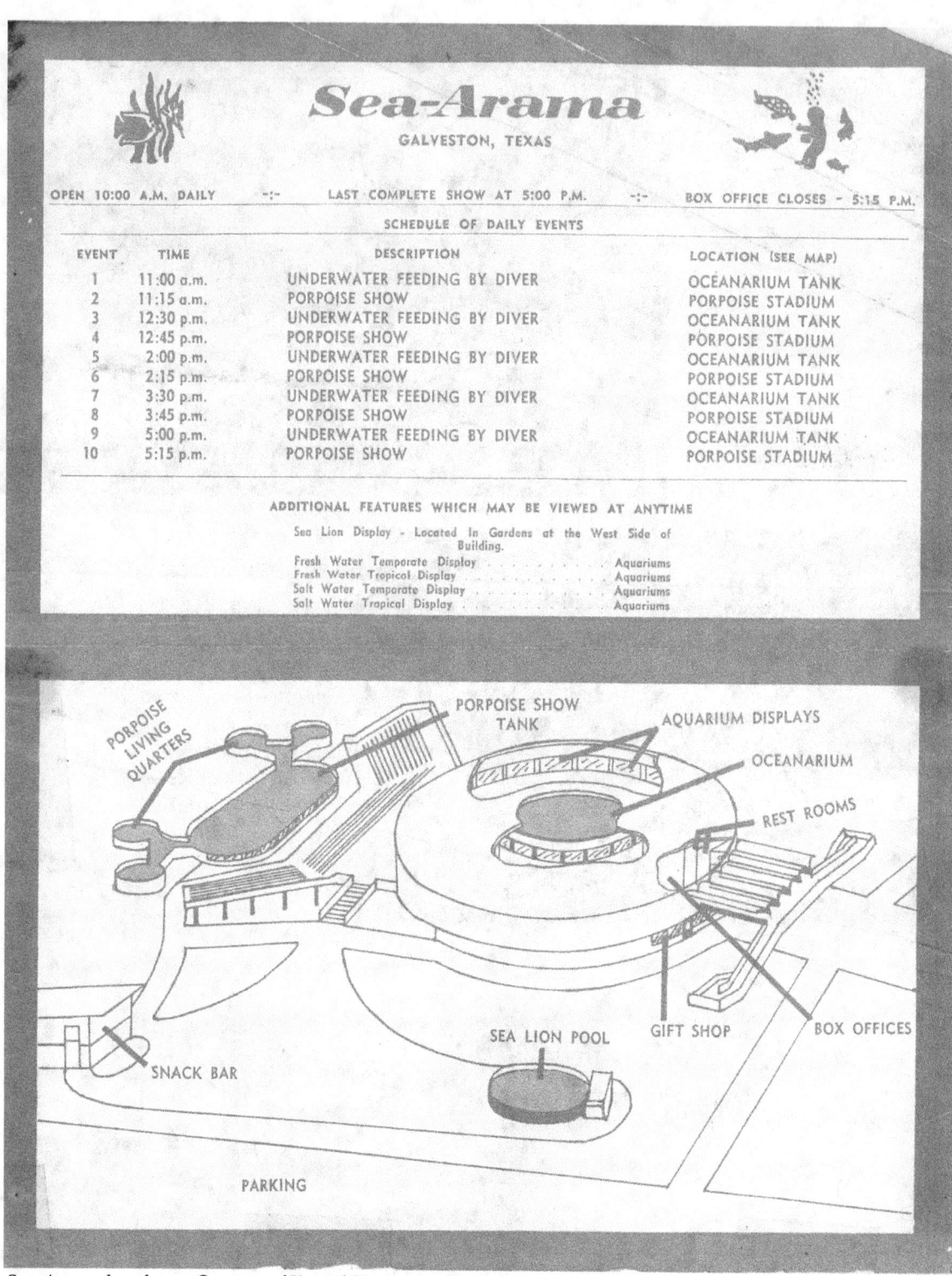

# Sea-Arama
### GALVESTON, TEXAS

OPEN 10:00 A.M. DAILY    -:-    LAST COMPLETE SHOW AT 5:00 P.M.    -:-    BOX OFFICE CLOSES - 5:15 P.M.

## SCHEDULE OF DAILY EVENTS

| EVENT | TIME | DESCRIPTION | LOCATION (SEE MAP) |
|-------|------|-------------|---------------------|
| 1 | 11:00 a.m. | UNDERWATER FEEDING BY DIVER | OCEANARIUM TANK |
| 2 | 11:15 a.m. | PORPOISE SHOW | PORPOISE STADIUM |
| 3 | 12:30 p.m. | UNDERWATER FEEDING BY DIVER | OCEANARIUM TANK |
| 4 | 12:45 p.m. | PORPOISE SHOW | PORPOISE STADIUM |
| 5 | 2:00 p.m. | UNDERWATER FEEDING BY DIVER | OCEANARIUM TANK |
| 6 | 2:15 p.m. | PORPOISE SHOW | PORPOISE STADIUM |
| 7 | 3:30 p.m. | UNDERWATER FEEDING BY DIVER | OCEANARIUM TANK |
| 8 | 3:45 p.m. | PORPOISE SHOW | PORPOISE STADIUM |
| 9 | 5:00 p.m. | UNDERWATER FEEDING BY DIVER | OCEANARIUM TANK |
| 10 | 5:15 p.m. | PORPOISE SHOW | PORPOISE STADIUM |

### ADDITIONAL FEATURES WHICH MAY BE VIEWED AT ANYTIME

Sea Lion Display - Located In Gardens at the West Side of Building.

| | |
|---|---|
| Fresh Water Temperate Display | Aquariums |
| Fresh Water Tropical Display | Aquariums |
| Salt Water Temperate Display | Aquariums |
| Salt Water Tropical Display | Aquariums |

Sea-Arama brochure. *Courtesy of Krystal Knutson.*

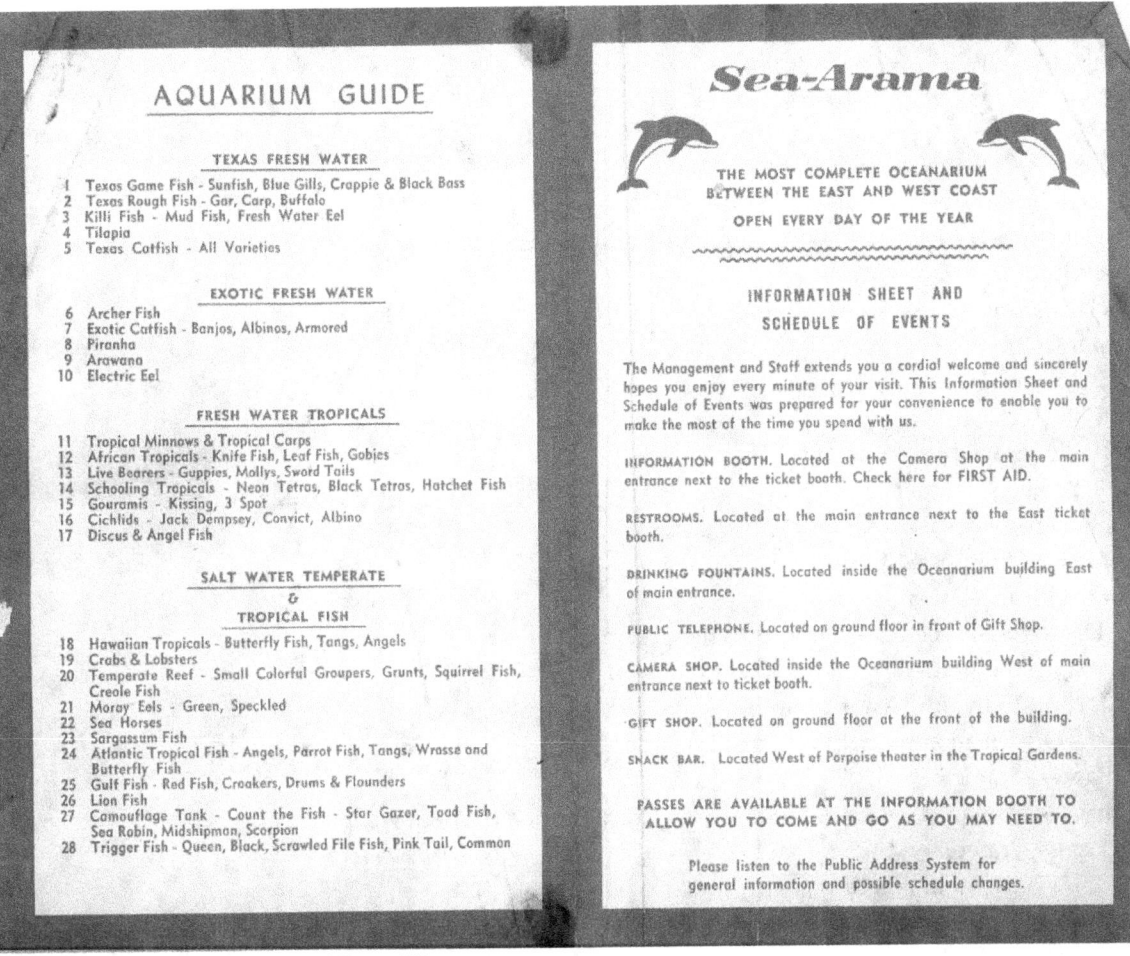

## AQUARIUM GUIDE

### TEXAS FRESH WATER

1. Texas Game Fish - Sunfish, Blue Gills, Crappie & Black Bass
2. Texas Rough Fish - Gar, Carp, Buffalo
3. Killi Fish - Mud Fish, Fresh Water Eel
4. Tilapia
5. Texas Catfish - All Varieties

### EXOTIC FRESH WATER

6. Archer Fish
7. Exotic Catfish - Banjos, Albinos, Armored
8. Piranha
9. Arawana
10. Electric Eel

### FRESH WATER TROPICALS

11. Tropical Minnows & Tropical Carps
12. African Tropicals - Knife Fish, Leaf Fish, Gobies
13. Live Bearers - Guppies, Mollys, Sword Tails
14. Schooling Tropicals - Neon Tetras, Black Tetras, Hatchet Fish
15. Gouramis - Kissing, 3 Spot
16. Cichlids - Jack Dempsey, Convict, Albino
17. Discus & Angel Fish

### SALT WATER TEMPERATE
### &
### TROPICAL FISH

18. Hawaiian Tropicals - Butterfly Fish, Tangs, Angels
19. Crabs & Lobsters
20. Temperate Reef - Small Colorful Groupers, Grunts, Squirrel Fish, Creole Fish
21. Moray Eels - Green, Speckled
22. Sea Horses
23. Sargassum Fish
24. Atlantic Tropical Fish - Angels, Parrot Fish, Tangs, Wrasse and Butterfly Fish
25. Gulf Fish - Red Fish, Croakers, Drums & Flounders
26. Lion Fish
27. Camouflage Tank - Count the Fish - Star Gazer, Toad Fish, Sea Robin, Midshipman, Scorpion
28. Trigger Fish - Queen, Black, Scrawled File Fish, Pink Tail, Common

## Sea-Arama

THE MOST COMPLETE OCEANARIUM
BETWEEN THE EAST AND WEST COAST

OPEN EVERY DAY OF THE YEAR

### INFORMATION SHEET AND
### SCHEDULE OF EVENTS

The Management and Staff extends you a cordial welcome and sincerely hopes you enjoy every minute of your visit. This Information Sheet and Schedule of Events was prepared for your convenience to enable you to make the most of the time you spend with us.

INFORMATION BOOTH. Located at the Camera Shop at the main entrance next to the ticket booth. Check here for FIRST AID.

RESTROOMS. Located at the main entrance next to the East ticket booth.

DRINKING FOUNTAINS. Located inside the Oceanarium building East of main entrance.

PUBLIC TELEPHONE. Located on ground floor in front of Gift Shop.

CAMERA SHOP. Located inside the Oceanarium building West of main entrance next to ticket booth.

GIFT SHOP. Located on ground floor at the front of the building.

SNACK BAR. Located West of Porpoise theater in the Tropical Gardens.

PASSES ARE AVAILABLE AT THE INFORMATION BOOTH TO ALLOW YOU TO COME AND GO AS YOU MAY NEED TO.

Please listen to the Public Address System for general information and possible schedule changes.

Sea-Arama brochure. *Courtesy of Krystal Knutson.*

## Some of the Animals:

Lafitte–porpoise
Squeaky–porpoise
Ki-Ko–porpoise
Trace–porpoise
Patty–porpoise
Black–porpoise
Sinbad–porpoise
Corky?–porpoise
Alvin (Al)–porpoise
Heidi–sea lion

Jocko-sea lion
Farouk-sea lion
Northern pike (fish)
Red tail catfish

Tim Gould

**Some of the employees:**
Ann Trent–Aquarist, curator
Belle Fenton–Gift shop manager
Ben Green–Diver
Bill Veale–Collector, diver
Bob Landers–Trainer
Bob Rutledge–Director of construction and maintenance
Brooks Robins–Trainer
Cheryl Beshears–Tickets, concessions
Chester Rollins–Diver
Clark Bowers–Head trainer
Dave McSpadden–Director of public relations
Denny Furchow–Head trainer
Dottie Samson–Trainer
Fred Eckert–General manager
Glenda Foster Snipes–Office secretary
Howard Picard–Diver
Jack Dismukes–Director of the corporation, board member
James (Jim) Bierman–Diver
James (Jim) Kelly, Jr.–Head curator
Jerry DeOrr–Head announcer and exhibit supervisor
Jim Parker–Trainer
Kathryn McDonald Taubert–Cashier during the summer, trainer by September
Ken Beggs–Trainer
Lee Kane–General manager
Lucille Ray–Landscaping
Mr. Miller–General manager
Randy Orkisch–Trainer
Teeny Kelly–Trainer
Tom Crauson–Trainer
Tom Whitman–Aquarist, curator
Travis Larue–Director

# 1967

In February 1967, the park added four new porpoises, which brought the total at Sea-Arama to eleven. Also in February, trainers introduced Heidi the sea lion into the porpoise show. By April the sea lions were a permanent part of the porpoise show; by the summer both Heidi and Farouk were performing their tricks with the porpoises.

The park saw the need for a covering over the porpoise stadium, so in June a pre-fabricated steel grandstand cover was installed to shelter 60 percent of the show seats.

November saw more animal acquisitions as six penguins from Peru were flown to Sea-Arama. The park was hoping to have them trained to ride roller skates and to dance within three to six months.

By early December the park was presenting the following shows and exhibits: Christmas porpoise revue, "Neptune's Noel," with costumes; "Dive to the Deep" in the Oceanarium; Sea Lion Show; Seven Seas Tour; and Tropical Gardens. The Seven Seas Tour was a new recorded narration of the 28 jewel tanks in the Oceanarium, while Tropical Gardens was a self-guided walk through the foliage and landscaping at Sea-Arama.

December 20, 1966, brought sad news: two of the six Humboldt penguins died from a fungal disease.

Kathryn McDonald Taubert and Heidi the sea lion. *Courtesy of Kathryn (Kathy) McDonald Taubert & digitization, courtesy of Robert Cubbage.*

Sea-Arama postcards of porpoise show. *Author's collection.*

Chester Rollins and Lafitte. Kathryn McDonald Taubert.

Farouk. *Courtesy of Kathryn (Kathy) McDonald Taubert & digitization, courtesy of Robert Cubbage.*

## Some of the employees:

Ann Trent–Aquarist, curator
Ben Green–Diver
Bill Veale–Collector, diver
Bob Landers–Trainer
Bob Rutledge–Director of construction and maintenance
Brooks Robins–Trainer
Cheryl Beshears–Tickets, concessions, mermaid or diver
Chester Rollins–Diver
Dave McSpadden–Public relations director
Denny Furchow–Head trainer
Dottie Samson–Trainer
Ed Moore–Executive vice president and general manager
Evan Larue Schaffer
Fred Eckert–General manager
Glenda Foster Snipes–Office secretary
Howard Picard–Diver, trainer of porpoises, whales, alligators
Jack Dismukes–Vice president of Sea-Arama Corporation

James (Jim) Bierman–Diver
James (Jim) Kelly, Jr.–Head curator
Jerry DeOrr–Announcer
Jim Parker–Training director as of April
Kathleen Stafford Sukiennik–Hostess, greeter, tickets, food bar, P.R.
Kathryn McDonald Taubert–Trainer
Ken Beggs–Trainer
Lucille Ray–Landscaping
Lee Kane–General manager
Michelle Moore–Concessions, ticket booth, gift shop
Mike Pistone–Custodian, cook, food/beverage supervisor
Mike Lemire–Trainer
Mr. Miller–General manager
Pete Fredriksen–Concession and cleanup crew
Randy Orkisch–Trainer
Rex Shield–President of the corporation
Ron Mozara–Diver, announcer, alligator wrestler
Steve O'Donohoe–Announcer
Teeny Kelly–Trainer

Tim Gould

Tom Crauson–Trainer
Tom Whitman–Aquarist, head curator
Travis Larue–Director
Vernette Mathews Porter–Balloon girl, gifts

**Some of the Animals:**

Lafitte–porpoise
Squeaky–porpoise
Ki-Ko–porpoise
Trace–porpoise
Patty–porpoise
Teeny–porpoise
Corky?–porpoise

Alvin (Al)–porpoise
Black–porpoise
Sinbad–porpoise
Heidi–sea lion
Farouk–sea lion
Jocko–sea lion
Six penguins

# 1968

Alligators were in Sea-Arama's future, and January saw the first alligator arrivals. The alligators were expected to be on display before May 1, with an alligator wrestling show to follow soon after.

Also in January, Governor John Connally toured Sea-Arama. Photos were taken of the governor shaking hands with Patty the porpoise.

In February, Otto the otter arrived. His training began for a hopeful participation in the Marineworld Revue porpoise show.

By March, scuba-outfitted, bikini-clad mermaids were doing ten scuba shows a day in the Oceanarium, where they performed underwater with sharks, sting rays, barracudas, and red fish. They did this after the regular diver had fed the fish. The mermaids also performed with a porpoise at the beginning of the Marineworld Revue.

In April 1968, Sea-Arama announced its plans for a $256,000 expansion program, which was to give Sea-Arama many new shows and exhibits as well as improved food facilities, air conditioning, an improved gift shop, and parking area improvements over the next four years. These would be the first major expansions since the park had opened (although the sea lion tank and snack bar were added more than a year earlier). This plan included:

— Whales: Sea-Arama's plan was to add at least one pilot whale to perform in the Marineworld Revue show. Sea-Arama hoped to allow guests to view the whales, when they were not in the Marineworld Revue, through half-inch-thick tempered polished plate glass that was mounted around the top edge of the holding pen.

— Octopus Grotto: The plan was to build this display to the northwest of the show stadium site.

— The Sea Lion exhibit. By April it was under construction. This was to take the place of, but be in a different location from, the current sea lion exhibit tank and would house Jocko and Samantha. The hope was to eventually create a sea lion theatre with waterfalls and slides.

— A future porpoise petting pool to the east of the show stadium. The plan was to add this exhibit in the future because of the many requests that Sea-Arama had received from its guests asking to touch and feed a porpoise.

— A future contact or petting zoo: This was becoming a favorite attraction throughout the U.S., so Sea-Arama planned to add a petting zoo as one of its new exhibits. This type of display would include an assortment of animals (ducks, sheep, lambs, rabbits, etc.) that children could pet and feed.

— The Marineworld Revue, which in April featured porpoises and sea lions, would be expanded to include the whales, an otter, and a penguin chorus line.

— A lagoon and waterfall were being constructed in the area of the original sea lion tank and snack bar. The plan was to have it landscaped and stocked with sharks in the lagoon and tropical birds in the land area, ultimately creating a new Tropical Garden.

— An alligator display pool had already been built next to the east ramp at the entrance. By April, it was already stocked with ten American alligators and one crocodile, including a 13-foot alligator (possibly the largest in Texas) in preparation for the future show.

— The Oceanarium was being remodeled with a new filtration system for better clarity.

— There were plans to add a space exhibit and an oceanographic exhibit.

— A revolving stage was to be added to the show stadium stage.

Of the many plans that were announced in 1968, some were carried out, some were not, and some were postponed. One that wasn't carried out was the slide. Sea-Arama announced that it would have its own gunny sack slide for visitors by May 1, 1968. It was to be built over two small lagoons on the park grounds, but for unknown reasons this never happened.

Other announced plans that were successful included the alligator show. In April, Sea-Arama showed the press a preview of the show; in May the alligator show opened to the public. The show part of this display included educational and interesting facts about the animals as well as alligator wrestling. The total cost of this display was $4,500.

Also in May, expansion of the Treasure Chest Gift Shop was underway, as well as construction of the Pirates Nook. Further additions to the food facilities would include the Pink Porpoise Ice Cream Parlor (to be completed by June 1). And, as of May, Sea-Arama became the first completely air-conditioned oceanarium-aquarium.

At this time the shows included the Seven Seas Tour of 28 jewel tanks, Dive to the Deep and scuba shows in the Oceanarium, alligator wrestling, and Marineworld Revue, which included sea lions joining the porpoises in attending "Porpoise Elementary School."

Sea-Arama added two bull sharks in the Oceanarium, totaling thirteen, in late spring. Because summer was a good time for adding more animals, Sea-Arama caught and added four new porpoises in June, bringing the total to nine. By the end of June Sea-Arama had acquired three new alligators, bringing their total to seventeen.

On June 22, Sea-Arama obtained its first whale from SeaWorld San Diego, trading seven bull sharks to SeaWorld for its 11-foot pilot whale, Nemo. At the time, this was the largest marine specimen exchange in history. Nemo was the first whale ever to be brought into Texas. One of Sea-Arama's favorite ads promoted its status as the only park between the east and west coasts to have a whale. The coastal parks that had a whale were the New York and Vancouver aquariums, the California and Florida Marinelands, and SeaWorld San Diego.

Also to come from SeaWorld San Diego, were two sea lions, four penguins, and a harbor seal (this information is unclear; it may have been three sea lions and two harbor seals). Sea-Arama sent in exchange five sharks, two six-foot stingrays, seventeen alligator gars, a five-foot green moray eel, two sawfish, eight spotted alligator gars, and two 300-pound spotted groupers (again, the information is unclear; it may have been six sharks and one spotted grouper).

Sea-Arama had recently completed a tank for Nemo located adjacent to the show tank. When he was placed in the whale tank, a porpoise was placed in the tank to keep him company, along with his toys.

This animal exchange was historic for another reason. Curators Tom Whitman of Sea-Arama and Dave Powell of SeaWorld had worked together to devise a mouthpiece to enable live transportation of the sharks. Before this time there was no way to keep these sharks alive for long transports because they had to have water running over their gills. The device they created enabled the sharks to breathe and allowed the animal exchange to be successful.

Nemo made his presence known at Sea-Arama on June 25, when he and his trainer, Jerry Foreman, were making the first trial run into the show stadium. The whale brushed against the half-inch glass windows of the show tank, breaking one. The result was 1,400 pounds of pilot whale and thousands of gallons of salt water rushing through the opening into the retaining pit in front of the show stadium. Nemo was washed to the other side of the retaining pit; he then turned around and swam back to the window where he had exited. He suffered head lacerations and a few bruises, but he was lifted back into the pool by trainers and other personnel, and he made a complete recovery in about two weeks.

By July the new Sea Lion Exhibit display and feeding show area was completed and ready for sea lions Jocko and Samantha. It had cost $21,000 and held 20,000 gallons of water. During the summer months there was a sea lion feeding show at this exhibit after trial runs of the feeding show in May.

August was a busy month. Sea-Arama completed the work on the Tropical Gardens display on the west side of the park, comprising a 13-foot waterfall, lagoon, and picnic area. The area was beautifully landscaped with exotic plants, small foot-trails winding throughout the gardens, and foot-bridges that crossed the lagoon.

That month one of the trainers, Howard Picard, was bitten by an alligator and wasn't able to perform for the remainder of the year. He received twenty-five stitches and it was feared he would lose the use of his hand. Picard had worked at Sea-Arama for three years and had also trained Lafitte the porpoise. He eventually recovered and continued his work at Sea-Arama and outside the park as a police officer.

Also in August, $6,000 worth of metal bars were installed around the show tank by the Sea-Arama construction crew to protect the show tank windows from whales and porpoises. The Octopus Grotto display was completed in August as well. This air-conditioned grotto held 1,000 gallons of water and cost $18,500.

September saw ten porpoises being added to Sea-Arama.

Many things happened in October. By this time Nemo had learned to jump up and touch a ball, brush his teeth (with the help of a trainer), talk, and roll over.

Sea-Arama hosted the Carbide Company Family Fun Days at Sea-Arama on October 5–6. Employees of the Carbide Company could take advantage of discount tickets to see new attractions such as the alligator show, Nemo, sea lion feeding show, and Otto the otter.

A further addition to Sea-Arama's food facilities in October was the completion of the Pirates Nook Restaurant, the Crow's Nest dining area, and the Pink Porpoise Ice Cream Parlor.

But by far Sea-Arama's biggest event to date occurred on October 29, when Mamuk arrived at Houston's Hobby Airport on his way to Sea-Arama. Once he was in his new home, he and Nemo were put together—briefly. Nemo rammed the larger Mamuk, so they were separated before Mamuk decided to hurt him. Trainers thought Nemo might be acting territorial toward the killer whale.

In December 1968 Heidi the sea lion, Nemo, penguins, and porpoises performed in a special Christmas show titled "Christmas around the World."

The new waterfall. *Courtesy of Dale Ware Family Archives.*

Left: Nemo, Sea-Arama's first whale. Right: Mamuk the Killer Whale. *Courtesy of James P. Kelly Jr.*

Tim Gould

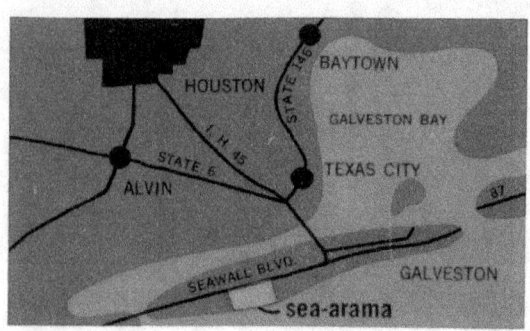

**LOCATION:** Sea-Arama Marineworld, on beautiful Galveston Island's West Beach is easily accessible by several major highways (see map). It is located at Seawall Boulevard and 91st Street, surrounded by the blue waters of the Gulf of Mexico and Galveston Bay. Large free parking area and only 25 minutes from Houston's International Airport.

**OPEN:** DAILY—Spring and Summer—10:00 a.m.-10:00 p.m. Fall and Winter—10:00 a.m.-Dusk Weekends and Holidays

**FACILITIES:** Sea-Arama Marineworld is the warmth—the friendliness—the face of youth, hiring most of its staff from the ranks of college and high school students. It is beautifully landscaped and immaculately clean. It is the world's most air conditioned marine park and features a covered stadium for your comfort. Sea-Arama Marineworld is especially beautiful at night. We feature the **Treasure Chest,** a most unique and complete gift and souvenir shop—we've been told it's the finest anywhere. And your family will love the **Pirate's Nook,** the highlight of our food facilities, surrounded by lush tropical gardens. And don't forget your camera! We will assist you in getting wonderful pictures and have complete film facilities at the **Shutter Shop.**

**ADMISSION:** Adults $2.25, Juniors (ages 12-17) $1.75, Children (ages 5-11) $1.25, Children under 5 FREE. One admission is all you pay to see all the shows and attractions at Sea-Arama Marineworld. Special prices for organized groups of 20 or more are available. For information contact the Sales Department or Public Relations Department at the address below:

A WORLD OF FAMILY FUN

**sea-Arama Marineworld**

Seawall Blvd. at 91st.—P. O. Box 869—Galveston, Texas

1968 Sea-Arama brochure. *Author's collection.*

106

## A World of Family Fun
## Sea-Arama Marineworld

Located on the West Beach of historic Galveston Island, Sea-Arama Marineworld is one of the most unique and complete multi-million dollar marine attractions in the world. It is the only attraction of its kind located between the east and west coasts.

Sea-Arama Marineworld's face is constantly changing with new shows, exhibits, and attractions being added seasonally. 1968 is certainly no exception with many great new shows being added featuring the only whales between the coasts. You'll see these "stars" as they're trained to take their roles in the unique Marineworld Revue. Other new features are alligator wrestling, a giant octopus, Otto the Performing Otter, penguin chorus line, sea lions, colorful birds and lush tropical gardens. The wonderful world of the sea is Sea-Arama Marineworld.

## A World of Fun and Amazement
## Marineworld Revue

Sea-Arama Marineworld presents three unique All-Star Marineworld Revues, Spring and Summer Revue, Fall and Winter Revue and the Special Christmas Revue each year. Written and produced by some of the country's most talented marine showmen, these shows include music, special sets, thematic scripts, costumes, and amazing feats performed by Sea-Arama Marineworld's fun loving porpoises, sea lions, whales, otters, penguins... and a few surprises—and a few surprises always mean more fun.

Whether you're 8, 18, or 80 you'll love the capricious, impish porpoise "stars" who are so intelligent you almost want to talk to them. And they'll tell you each time you visit us... it's always SHOW TIME AT SEA-ARAMA MARINEWORLD.

## The World of the Seven Seas
## Seven Seas Tour

Almost like magic you and your family are transported to the seven sea-wonders of the world. You become involved in the mystery, the utter fascination, the unbelievable beauty of the marine society of the depths. Specimens collected throughout the world by Sea-Arama Marineworld make their home here... including: Moray Eels, Lobsters, Trigger Fish, Sea Horses, Sea Anemones, Batfish, Cannibalistic Piranha, Australian Lung Fish, Arawona, Ebue Eel, Northern Pike, Sturgeon, Wall Eyed Pike, Red Tailed Catfish, Arapaima, Large Mouth Bass, Alligator Gar, Quill Back, Colossama, Shovel Nosed Catfish, Tiger Catfish, Archer Fish, Queensland Grouper, Toad Fish, Sail Fin Tang, Pompanos, Sea Robin, Common Butterfly Fish, Parrot Fish, Octopus, Red Snapper, Electric Eels, Nurse Shark, Torpedo Ray... and many more. The Seven Seas Jewel Aquarium Tour is a world of interesting facts and strange sights with many specimens not on display anywhere else in the United States. We are proud of the fact that we have been rated as having one of the very best aquarium tours in the world. It's your world to see from the Seven Seas.

## A World of Mystery and Excitement
## Dive to the Deep Show

You are transported into the mystery and excitement of the deep sea diver's world in Sea-Arama Marineworld's Dive to the Deep Oceanarium Show. Through 32 huge viewing ports you'll see the never ending drama of large and dangerous sea creatures living together in our 160,000 gallon recreated ocean home. You'll see unpredictable man-eating Sharks, deadly Sting Rays, Barracudas, giant Spotted Groupers (one weighing-in at over 600 pounds, considered the largest living fish in captivity), huge 6 ft. Moray Eels, giant Sea Turtles, Alligator Gars and many more deadly and exciting salt water fish. At times you may see an underwater fight for survival. You'll witness the fascinating spectacle of many of these creatures of the deep being hand-fed by Sea-Arama Marineworld's specially trained divers.

"Utterly fascinating... very interesting." These are the most often heard quotes from our visitors from the world over. You and your family will thrill to the mystery and excitement of the "Dive to the Deep."

1968 Sea-Arama brochure. *Author's collection.*

**Some of the employees:**

Ann Trent?–Aquarist, curator
Bobby Andresakis?–Snakes, alligators
Bob Landers–Trainer
Bob Rutledge–Director of park operation
Cheryl Beshears–Tickets, concessions, mermaid or diver
Diane Wilson–Mermaid
Doyle Wolfe–Director of engineering and construction
Ed Moore–General manager
Foster Spurkock
Howard Picard–Assistant training director for alligators, whales, porpoises
Jack Dismukes–Vice president of Sea-Arama Corporation
James Watts–Food court manager
Jay Paxson–Diver (later did alligators and snakes)
Jerry Foreman–Training director (came in Jan '68)
Jim Parker–Training director
Jimmie Sommerfield–Janitor, alligators, snakes
Joan Cole Wallace
Joe Mayhew–Assistant curator
Kathleen Stafford Sukiennik–Hostess, greeter, tickets, food bar, P.R.

Lucille Ray–Landscaping
Mike McNabb–Public relations
Michelle Moore–Concessions, ticket booth, gift shop
Mike Pistone–Custodian, cook, food/beverage supervisor
Ron Mozara–Diver, announcer, alligator wrestler
Ross Eliason–Diver, skier, snakes, and rode on the killer whale during shows
Shirley Paxson–Food concession booth
Sidney R Kay–Veterinarian
Stan Schreiber–Sales director, announcer
Steve O'Donohoe–Promoted April '68 to live show director
Susie Ahern Knust–Whale & Seahorse bars, Pirates Nook, Ski Hut, Pink Porpoise, Petting Zoo
Terry Moore–Landscaping and trainer
Tom Whitman–Curator
Toni Lera–Oceanarium mermaid
Vernette Mathews Porter–Balloon girl, gift shop
Wendy Fesler Millo–Gift shop

**Some of the Animals:**

Lafitte–porpoise
Trace–porpoise
Squeaky–porpoise
Ki-Ko–porpoise
Corky?–porpoise
Patty–porpoise
Alvin (Al)–porpoise
Black–porpoise
Sinbad–porpoise
Mamuk–killer whale
Nemo–pilot whale
Samantha–sea lion

Heidi–sea lion
Otto–North American otter
Hubert–penguin
Oscar–penguin
Gertrude–penguin
Gladys–penguin
17 alligators by July
Harbor seal
Moray eels
Lobsters
Trigger fish
Sea horses

# Sea-Arama Marineworld

Sea anemones
Batfish
Piranha
Australian lung fish
Arawona
Ebue eel
Northern pike
Sturgeon
Wall eyed pike
Red tailed catfish
Arapaima
Largemouth bass
Alligator gar
Quill back
Colossama
Shovel nosed catfish
Tiger catfish
Archer fish
Queensland grouper
Toad fish
Sail fin tang

Pompanos
Sea robin
Common butterfly fish
Parrot fish
Octopus
Red snapper
Electric eels
Nurse shark
13 bull sharks
Torpedo ray
Sting rays
Barracudas
Giant spotted groupers
Giant sea turtles

# 1969

In February of 1969 Sea-Arama continued its four-phased remodeling plan.

- Whales: Sea-Arama now had two whales and desired to add them to the Marineworld Revue first and eventually have their own show. Mamuk was being trained, and the public could view his training sessions (Nemo was already part of the show).

- Marineworld Revue: The penguins had joined the revue in December for the special Christmas show, but the plans were for them to become a permanent part of the show. Sea-Arama had been training a team of four Humboldt penguins from Peru and was expecting four more. The park hoped that the penguins Hubert, Oscar, Gertrude, and Gladys would delight audiences as Gladys perched in the crow's nest of a five-foot pirate ship pulled by one of the porpoises. The penguins would be housed in a special display so that guests could see them when they weren't in the revue. Also being added to the revue were a new stage set, costumes, music, and new scripts. Total cost would be $3,000.

- Park Grounds: To further enhance the front entrance, visitors entering Sea-Arama now walked over the lagoon on a special walkway resembling the boarding ramp of a ship. The lagoon varied in width from 20 to 50 feet and was approximately 300 feet long. It also remodeled its front entrance to bring its ticket windows and guest relations headquarters to the ground level.

There were new things on the horizon for Sea-Arama in March of 1969:

- The existing alligator wrestling show was going to be moved to its new island

- location, and Jean Lafitte's Raft Ride was going to take guests across the water ski area to the Alligator Island. Plans called for Tom Sawyer-type rafts powered by 40hp outboard motors.

- Plans were to replace the alligator display with an exotic bird display featuring flamingoes, egrets, swans, ibises, pelicans, and ducks.

- The Oleander Garden was being designed in cooperation with the National Oleander Society.

- The existing sea lion tank was to be modified for a harbor seal show, with the seals trained to do different tricks for food, and public feedings of the animals.

- Plans were to create a new marine pet shop at the front entrance due to the interest generated by Sea-Arama's aquarium displays. Guests would be able to purchase exotic fish, alligators, and other aquatic species. The curating department would offer help to people setting up a home aquarium.

- Sea-Arama also planned to upgrade the existing sound systems and to add background and sound effects for all shows.

- A new Marineworld Revue theme was planned that involved a humorous salute to the Apollo space program, written around the idea of what man may find on the moon.

- A TV special called "Nemo the Flying Whale" — Channel 11 came up with a documentary special on the true story of how Nemo the pilot whale was caught, transported from California to Texas by air, and then taught to do various tricks at Sea-Arama.

- It was announced that Mamuk eventually would be moved to the large lake at the front of the property. This new show area would be 250 by 200 feet and would be the largest area in which any killer whale in the world performed. It would have 1.5 million cubic feet of water with a depth of thirty feet. A thirty to thirty-five-minute show was planned for the killer whale, including pulling water skiers and a jump off a ski jump of twenty or more feet. Sea-Arama planned to have more than one killer whale, and it was hoped with the larger body of water, Mamuk would continue to grow and would become the largest killer whale in captivity.

In April the water ski show premiered. By summer, the 30-minute ski show was performed four to six times daily.

On May 23, John Kalb, winner of the 1968 Orange Bowl 250 Speed Classic and veteran driver for the Mecom Racing Team, made an appearance at Sea-Arama. Kalb even took a ride on Mamuk's back.

On July 11, the new $40,000 alligator and crocodile island opened. The moving of twenty-five alligators and three crocodiles from their old enclosure to their new island home had taken place the previous week, with no injuries to people or animals. A dragline had to be employed in the moving of several of the larger alligators weighing in excess of 700 pounds.

Also by July, three new shows were up and running: the whale show, harbor seal show, and water ski show. Still under construction were the pirate raft ride, Oleander Garden, and exotic bird display.

The new whale show had begun as killer whale training sessions and developed into a killer whale show where, in addition to other tricks, Mamuk let one of four mermaids ride on his back. Mamuk was seen by visitors five times a day in his show and training sessions. He was kept in the whale tank, while Nemo lived in the show tank. During the porpoise show, Nemo was put in the flume between the show tank and the whale tank.

By August there were numerous changes:

- The completion of the exotic/coastal bird display at the former alligator tank location. Flamingos would be brought in later.

- The Polynesian motif for the park was about half done.

- The original plans for 1969 were to include the pirate raft ride and pet shop, but both have been put off until 1970.

- There was a new backdrop for the porpoise stadium that depicted a porpoise elementary school.

- The porpoise stadium had been fully covered (instead of just the middle section) with a metal roof, and the stage area has been closed off from the animals' holding pools.

- A new, air-conditioned animal house had been added for the four penguins and the sea lions and seals housed there. The eight pens inside included one for Heidi the sea lion.

- The Octopus Grotto, added the previous year, was being changed to add more invertebrates and two new, small aquarium exhibits.

By September:

- Another animal addition was Annie the chimpanzee, who had not worked her way into a show yet.

- In his show, Nemo went through the routine of a kid on his first day at school. Nemo's act included the high jump, retrieving objects, being examined by a doctor, and playing baseball.

In October, there was talk of the mermaids retiring from riding Mamuk because Sea-Arama was afraid they would be accidentally crushed by the whale. Trainer Jerry Foreman was doing most of the whale riding now.

In November 1969, Ross Allen, president of the National Crocodilian Society, was brought to Sea-Arama to advise the curators in the care, training, and handling of the animals. Mr. Allen had worked as a stunt man and animal handler in more than 125 movies, including the Tarzan films that starred Johnny Weissmuller.

Pirate's Ski Adventure

An All Tom Corp. postcard. *Author's collection.*

Bobby Andresakis during the alligator show. *Courtesy of Greg May.*

Porpoises Patty and Corky in June 1969. *Courtesy of James P. Kelly Jr.*

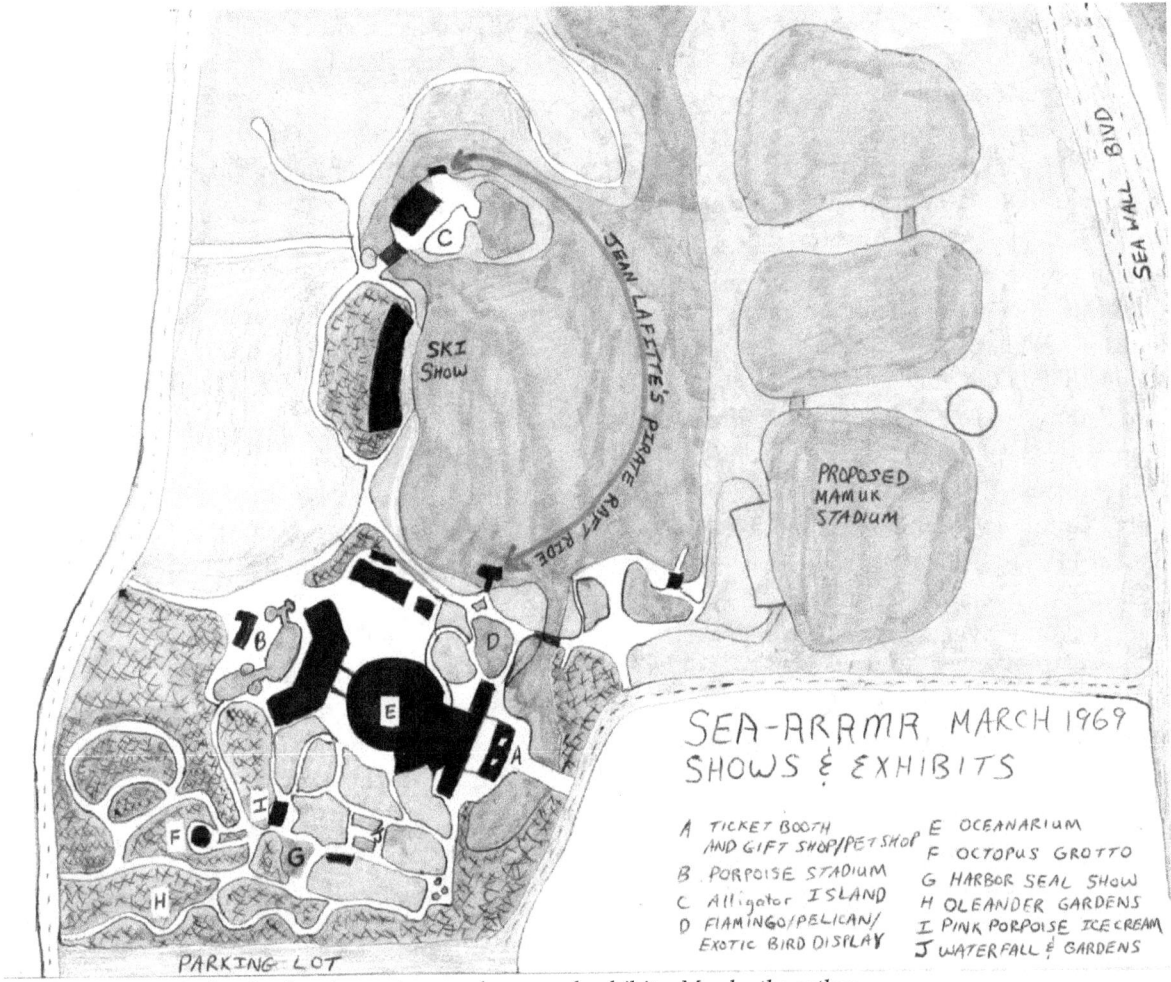

March 7 proposed plan for Sea-Arama's new shows and exhibits. *Map by the author.*

**Some of the employees:**

Ann Trent–Aquarist, curator
Bill Klontz–Veterinarian
Bill Moody–Board member
Bill Rochelle–Director of sales and special events
Bobby Andresakis–Snakes, alligators
Bob Crain–Announcer
Bob Landers–Trainer
Cathy Carter?–Skier
Chris Dougherty–Secretary of Sea-Arama Corporation
Clarence Pleasants–Director of landscaping
Cliff Townsend–Board member

Diane Wilson–Mermaid
Dick Sharper–Curator
Doyle Wolfe–Director of engineering and construction
Dudley Anderson–Director of food and concessions
Ed Moore–Executive vice president and general manager
Gary (Bubba) Brandenberger–Skier
Greg Scofelia–Skier
Henry Ramsey–Treasurer of Sea-Arama Corporation
Howard Picard–Alligators, whales, porpoises

Jack Dismukes–Vice president of Sea-Arama Corporation
Jack Hammit–Skier
Jack Scarbrough–Board member
James Watts–Food court manager
Jay Paxson–Diver, alligators, snakes
Jerry Foreman–Training director, whales, alligators, porpoises
Jimmie Sommerfield–Janitor, alligators, snakes
Joan Cole Wallace
John Hill–Board member
John Humason (Doc Rail)–Ski show director
John Schwebel–Director of Concessions
John Simpson–Chairman of the board
Judy Plantowsky–Mermaid
Howard Picard–Alligators, whales
Ken Gray–Associate veterinarian
Ken Yoakum–Diver, alligator wrestler, head diver in late '60s
Leslie Shupe Borsellino–Whale Bar, Seahorse, Pirates Nook, Ski Hut, Pink Porpoise, Petting Zoo
Mark Ward–Curator of alligators
Melanie Guckian Ping? –Skier
Melissa McClellan–Mermaid, skier
Michelle Moore–Concessions, ticket booth, gift shop
Mike McNabb–Public relations director
Mike Pistone–Custodian, cook, food/beverage supervisor

Paul McGee–Curator
Rex Shields–President of Sea-Arama Corporation
Rhonda Demetrios–Skier
Robert Carmouche (stage name Bob Crain)–Announcer
Ron Mozara–Diver, announcer, alligator wrestler
Ross Eliason–Diver, skier, snakes, and rode on the killer whale during shows
Sam Martinez–Janitor, alligators, snakes
Shirley Paxson–Food concession booth
Steve Harris–Skier
Steve O'Donohoe–Director of live shows
Susie Ahern Knust–Whale Bar, Seahorse, Pirates Nook, Ski Hut, Pink Porpoise, Petting Zoo
Terry Moore–Trainer, whales, alligators
Tom Whitman–Curator
Travis LaRue–Board member
Vernette Mathews Porter–Balloon girl, gift shop
Wayne Esserman–Skier
Wayne Moore–Board member
Wendy Fesler Millo–Gift shop

**Some of the Animals:**
Lafitte–porpoise
Patty–porpoise
Squeaky–porpoise
Ki-Ko–porpoise
Corky–porpoise
Trace–porpoise
Alvin (Al)–porpoise
Black–porpoise
Sinbad–porpoise

Over 25 porpoises, including:
Heidi–sea lion
Jocko–sea lion
Baby–harbor seal
Mamuk–killer whale
Nemo–pilot whale
Annie–chimpanzee
Penguins
Alligators
Octopus

# 1970

The year 1970 was significant for Sea-Arama in good ways and bad. Some big shows and exhibits were added, and some big animals were acquired and, unfortunately, died.

By February the park landscaping had been greatly improved:

- Tropical birds had been added to the Tropical Gardens, along with two hand-carved tikis, the largest one reaching sixteen feet tall.

- Fifty palm trees, Polynesian bridges, fountains, waterfalls, torches, and wooden bridges were added.

- Plans were announced to raise two sunken ships, both 45-feet long, to be placed at different areas throughout the park.

- More than 4,500 specimens of plants were brought in from all over the world, including palms, eucalyptus, Australian pine, and rubber plants.

- Sea-Arama had planned to have sharks swimming in the lagoon, but that didn't work out.

On April 30, Sea-Arama had its first major tragedy when Nemo the pilot whale died from liver failure, compounded by pneumonia.

Sea-Arama rebounded quickly; by May the park was announcing new shows and displays, which included:

- The new snake display and snake show. The snakes were added to the existing alligator show in April. A couple of months after this, the snake display was completed.

- New seal and sea lion feeding and show area. In May, this feature was being constructed in a converted area just to the east of the front entrance. Ten seals and seven sea lions would be featured, along with the penguins and other exotic birds nearby. The park planned to eventually add music and costumes to create a show for the seals and sea lions in this area.

- Tomb of the Lost Dolphin. This site would soon be one of the most exciting of the new displays and would be part of the existing Octopus Grotto.

- Deer petting park. New for this year would be the deer petting park (later called the petting zoo), located adjacent to the Octopus Grotto. The previous plan had been to add this attraction in 1971, but the park moved up the date to 1970 instead. Kids would be able to play with and feed goats, burros, baby deer, llamas, and other animals.

- Sea anemone display. Added to the Octopus Grotto, along with the Tomb of the Lost Dolphin, was a sea anemone petting pool, housed in a curving glass display tank with an artificial indoor waterfall.

- Porpoise petting area, which had been in development for two years.

- Pirates raft ride, taking visitors into a fog-covered land of mystery in the alligator and snake show area.

- A new Garden of the Gods by the tikis.

- An expansion of the alligator stadium.

- A new ski show with a circus theme.

- A new killer whale rodeo show called "The Last Round Up."

- Major changes in the mermaid/scuba show in the Oceanarium.

- A new script for the porpoise show.

By June a new attraction had opened, while other exhibits were making progress. The new attraction was the long-awaited Jean Lafitte's Raft Ride, which used two barges to carry people to Alligator Island. The porpoise petting pool and the petting zoo were complete and awaiting additional animals. The snake display was 90 percent finished; the seal and sea lion feeding pool was 80 percent finished, but visitors could still visit both areas. The Tomb of the Lost Dolphin and the sea anemone petting pool were about half finished and not ready for public viewing yet.

At the end of June, Sea-Arama added an 800-pound animal to the park in the form of Fat Albert the elephant seal. He was to be trained for another new show in September.

In 1970, Sea-Arama was an extraordinary place to visit. A typical day for a visitor in June of 1970 would include touring the large main building with its gift shop and restaurants on the ground floor and Oceanarium on its second level, along with enjoying the half-hour killer whale show and the half-hour porpoise show (which included a sea lion and two penguins who went down a slide). Audiences could see porpoises Patty, Squeaky, Lafitte, Al, Trace, Black, Sinbad, Kiko, Corky, and Lucy as they did their leaps and high jumps through hoops, put out fires, and passed footballs to their handlers. Mamuk performed in his Texas-style rodeo show where he jumped twelve feet out of the water and ended the show by splashing the audience.

At the Oceanarium, the public could watch mermaids and divers swimming among and feeding hundreds of dangerous fish, sharks, sting rays, and eels, as well as a demonstration of scuba equipment, spear fishing, and hazards of the deep. Visitors could view the twenty-two jewel tanks housing stone fish, lion fish, and piranha, and they could enjoy watching the ski show performers in the "Greatest Show on Water."

In the eastern section of the park, the visitor could view the reptile show, gasping when trainer Bobby Andresakis bare-handed a venomous hooded cobra and wrestled a huge alligator with his back-up man Sam Martinez. Other sites to see were the snake display, petting zoo, waterfall, and bird display.

On August 20, Sea-Arama's second killer whale, Nooka, arrived from Seattle via plane and truck. The twelve-foot youngster had been captured two weeks earlier along with sixty other killer whales in the largest catch to date. He was chosen because his youth would make him easier to train and keep healthy. His name meant "little brother" in the Eskimo–Aleut language. When he arrived at Sea-Arama he was placed in the same holding tank as Mamuk to help him acclimate to his new home. The hope was to have them both performing by the next spring. Work had begun on the new whale stadium in the previous year, but Sea-Arama knew it would have to complete the work quickly because of the size and needs of the two animals. The park projected that the stadium would be ready by the end of the year.

In October the Vancouver Aquarium sent two harbor seals to be used in the mermaid/scuba show in the Oceanarium.

By November Sea-Arama was on its winter schedule, only open on weekends and school holidays from November 5 to March 1. It used this time off to be able to train the animals.

Bobby Andresakis during the snake show. *Courtesy of Greg May.*

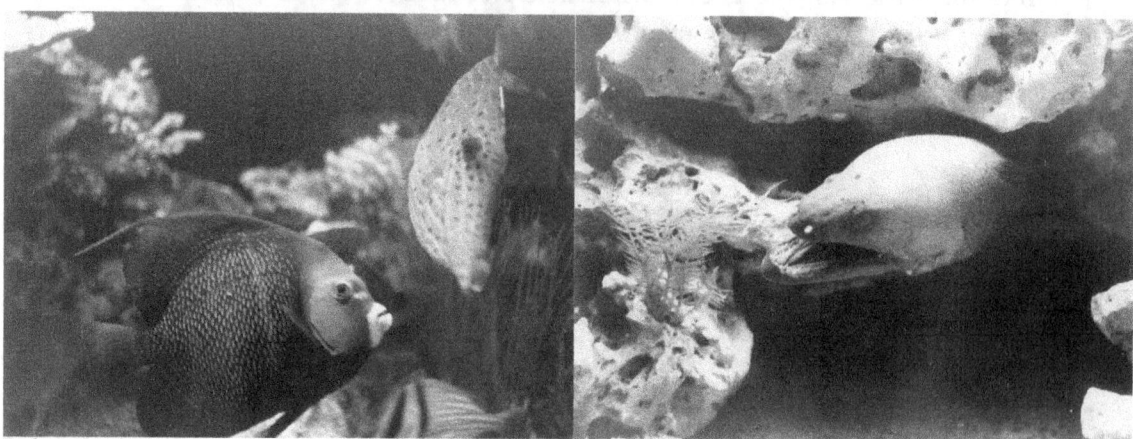

Fish and eel in the Oceanarium. *Courtesy of Greg May*

Sea-Arama Marineworld

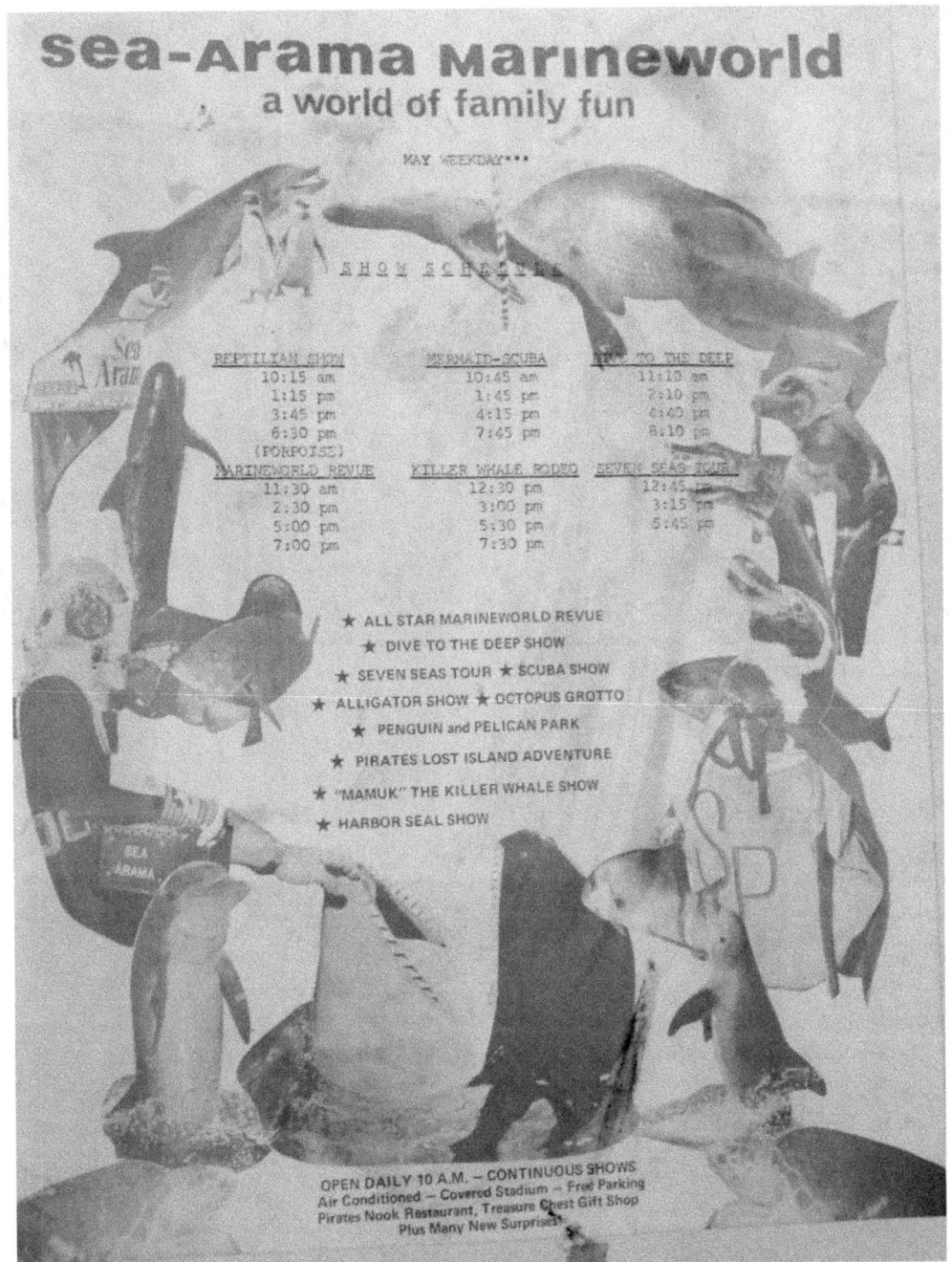

Show schedule circa 1970. *Author's collection.*

*Colorful Permanent Residents*

Macaws. *Author's collection.*

**Some of the employees:**

Al Pavone–Skier
Ann Trent–Aquarist, curator
Bill Klontz–Veterinarian
Bryan Springer
Bobby Andresakis–Snakes, alligators
Bob Landers–Trainer
Candi Hughes–Food court, gift shop, ski show, mermaid
Clarence Pleasants–Director of landscaping
Crystal Spangberg–Skier
Cynthia Barr–Mermaid
Dr. Bill Klontz–Veterinarian
Debra Hughes Weaver–Food court, gift shop, ski show, mermaid
Diane Flores Cowart–Food court, gift shop, ski show kites/skier
Don Leberman–Reptile specialist

Ed Moore–Executive vice president and general manager
George Ulrich–Skier
Grant Fratt–Alligators
Greg Scofelia–Skier
Hal Newsom?–Alligators, diver, snakes
Jack Hammit–Skier
James Watts–Food Court Manager
Jerry Foreman–Training Director
Jimmie Sommerfield–Janitor, alligators, snakes
Joan Cole Wallace
Joan Jefferies–Skier
John Humason (Doc Rail)–Ski show director
Ken Gray–Associate veterinarian
Leslie Shupe Borsellino–Whale Bar, Seahorse, Pirates Nook, Ski Hut, Pink Porpoise, Petting Zoo

## Sea-Arama Marineworld

Mark Johnson–Skier
Marsha Mullins–Skier
Melissa McClellan–Mermaid, ski show
Michelle Moore–Concessions, ticket booth, gift shop
Mike McNabb–Public relations director
Mike Pistone–Custodian, cook, food/beverage supervisor
Paula Trost–Mermaid '70–'72, assistant curator to veterinarian
Perry Blackwell–Announcer
Renee Rodgers–Skier
Rhonda Demetrios–Skier
Richard Biffle–Skier
Sam Martinez–Janitor, alligators, snakes

Shelly Demetrios–Skier
Starla Terry–Skier
Steve O'Donohoe–Director of live shows
Steve Harris–Skier
Susan Minter Medford–Skier
Susie Ahern Knust–Whale Bar, Seahorse, Pirates Nook, Ski Hut, Pink Porpoise, Petting Zoo
Terry Moore–Trainer, whales, alligators
Vernette Mathews Porter–Balloon girl, gift shop
Wayne Esserman–Skier
Wendy Fesler Millo–Gift shop

### Some of the Animals:
Lafitte–porpoise
Squeaky–porpoise
Ki-Ko–porpoise
Trace–porpoise
Corky–porpoise
Patty–porpoise
Alvin (Al)–porpoise
Black–porpoise
Sinbad–porpoise
Lucy–porpoise
Heidi–sea lion

Fat Albert–elephant seal
Mamuk–killer whale
Nooka–killer whale
Nemo–pilot whale
Baby deer
Llama
Sea anemones
Burros
Snakes
Goats
Tropical/exotic birds

# 1971

The completion of two new exhibits was the highlight of the beginning of 1971.

- The Garden of the Gods allowed visitors to sit at dining tables surrounding the garden patio area just outside the Tiki Hut snack bar. Visitors could picnic on the grass around the lost lagoon or stand below the waterfall and feed the exotic birds.

- The wooden Polynesian bridge at the seal and sea lion feeding pool was completed. It crossed the pond, which allowed visitors to feed the seals and sea lions below.

By February, Mamuk was becoming too large to travel from his holding area into the show tank. The flume or passageway had to be enlarged four feet in width and two feet in depth. Workmen began jackhammering on a Sunday night because of only a five-day working time. They had to work around the clock to complete the project in time for the weekend performances. Most of the water was drained from the show and holding tanks where sixteen porpoises also lived.

Future expansion plans included more than $150,000 for additions to the park in 1971. An all new whale stadium and Mamuk show, with little brother Nooka was estimated to be completed by June 1972, at a cost of $300,000. Sea-Arama planned to eventually have three killer whales.

Sea-Arama saluted the 61st birthday of the Boy Scouts of America with its third annual "Salute to Boy Scouts" in February. All the scout leaders got into the park for a reduced price of $1.75 on Friday, Saturday, and Sunday, and all scouts received a free embroidered "Mamuk the Killer Whale" patch. For the first time in scout history, Ft. Smith, Arkansas, Ardmore, Oklahoma, Monroe, and New Orleans were participating in the salute.

In early March, Sea-Arama returned to a seven-day-a-week operation, and in 1971 Sea-Arama made a commitment to stay open year-round. Also in March, Sea-Arama advertised a new future show to be called Noah's Ark and an expanded killer whale show with both killer whales coming in the summer.

Later in March, another Sea-Arama tragedy struck when Lil Nooka died of asphyxiation. He was approximately three years old when he died March 18.

On March 22, the launching of Noah's ark into the water occurred. It was 57 feet long, 27 feet long, and weighed 20 tons. It took a giant crane and a crew of six men to launch it, but during launching the stern broke off. The hope was to have the show premiere on June 1 of 1971.

At some point in 1971, Ollie the octopus was stolen in the middle of the night, which mean that Sea-Arama had to buy another octopus.

In August eight alligators were given to Sea-Arama by the DOW Company.

Crocodile. *Courtesy of Greg May.*

Killer Whale Show. *Courtesy of*
*www.vintagevacationphotos.com.*

Killer Whale Show. *Courtesy of*
*www.vintagevacationphotos.com.*

Jon Littmann on Mamuk the Killer Whale. *Courtesy of Jon Littmann.*

Bobby Andresakis with a 13-foot alligator.

Sea lion and seal feeding bridge. *Courtesy of Dale Ware Family Archives.*

Shark in the Oceanarium. *Courtesy of Greg May.*

**Some of the employees:**
Ann Trent–Aquarist, curator
Bill Klontz–Veterinarian
Bobby Andresakis–Snakes, alligators
Bob Landers–Trainer
Bryan Springer
Bryce Scherner–Skier
Anthony John (Bubba) Forester–skier
Candi Hughes–Food, gift shop, ski, mermaid
Clarence Pleasants–Director of landscaping
Crystal Spangberg–Skier
Debbie Lilly Autry–Skier
Debbie McKinley Williams–Skier
Debra Hughes Weaver–Food, gifts, ski, mermaid
Dell Harkey–Skier
Diane Flores Cowart–Food, gifts, ski, kites
Dick Waterman–Director of special events
Ed Moore–Executive VP and GM
Ginny Bland–Skier
Greg Scofelia–Skier
Hal Newsom?–Alligators, diver, snakes
James Watts–Food court manager
Jeff Brown–Skier
Jimmie Sommerfield–Janitor, alligators, snakes
Jimmy Watson–Animal collector
Joan Cole Wallace
John Braunsdorf–Skier
John Humason (Doc Rail)–Ski show director
Jon Littmann–1960s maintenance & construction, 1971 & '72 announcer
Ken Gray–Operations manager/veterinarian

Kyle Janek–Gift shop
Leslie Shupe Borsellino–Whale Bar, Seahorse, Pirates Nook, Ski Hut, Pink Porpoise, Petting Zoo
Mary Eggleston–Skier
Mark Johnson–Skier
Melissa McClellan–Mermaid, skier
Michelle Moore–Concessions, tickets, gift shop
Mike McNabb–Public relations director
Mike Pistone–Custodian, cook, food/beverage supervisor
Paula Trost–Mermaid '70–'72, assistant curator for veterinarian
Perry Blackwell–Alligators, snakes
Richard Biffle–Skier
Rick Glover–Diver, merman, alligator wrestler, lawn maintenance
Ronnie Ginsberg–Skier
Roy Garza–Alligators, snakes
Sandy Boudreaux Scardino–Gift shop
Sherri Peck Aymes–Mermaid
Starla Terry–Skier
Steve O'Donohoe–Director of live shows
Steve Harris–Ski lead
Susan Minter Medford–Ski lead
Susie Ahern Knust–Whale Bar, Seahorse, Pirates Nook, Ski Hut, Pink Porpoise, Petting Zoo
Terry Moore–Ski lead
Vernette Mathews Porter–Balloon girl, gifts
Wayne Esserman–Skier
Wendy Fesler Millo–Gift shop

**Some of the Animals:**
Lafitte, Trace, Squeaky–porpoise
Ki-Ko–porpoise
Corky–porpoise
Lucy–porpoise
Heidi–sea lion
Barnaby–seal

Fat Albert–elephant seal
Mamuk–killer whale
Lil Nooka–killer whale
Ollie–octopus
Alligators

# 1972

The year 1972 marked the largest attendance ever at Sea-Arama, with 404,833 people visiting the park. This year there was a new look: "pirate theme in a south-seas setting."

On January 20 the 103-foot schooner *Southwind* made its way over land to Sea-Arama after being raised out of Galveston Bay, where it had rested after sinking. It took one week to move it 16 miles to the park.

In February, Jimmie Sommerfield spent several days in the hospital recuperating from a diamondback rattler bite on the foot during the snake show. Unfortunately, he lost half of his foot in the recovery process.

Within the past year, Dr. Ken Gray had been added officially to the Sea-Arama staff. He would lay the groundwork for a comprehensive program of research on marine mammals and their diseases. He would also develop Sea-Arama's scientific program in conjunction with the Texas A&M University's staff and facilities in this field.

April 1 was the scheduled opening for the new ski show, "The Wild Wet West," a spoof of many favorite Western characters. Then, on May 15 came the official opening of the new Noah's Ark show.

There was a common practice of putting a Sea-Arama bumper sticker on every car in the parking lot. After receiving complaints about this, Executive Vice President and General Manager Ed Moore discontinued the practice in June.

In the fall of 1972, alligator and snake handler Bobby Andresakis announced that he would soon be leaving Sea-Arama. He would be trading in his alligator pants for a deep-sea diving suit after deciding that switching professions was a good idea because there really wasn't a future in alligator wrestling. His wife Paula was reported to be very pleased with this decision.

The December Christmas show in 1972 was "Little Orphan Porpoise" featuring Mamuk, sea lions, and Tiny Tina (one of the porpoises).

*Southwind* on the Galveston Seawall, on its way to Sea-Arama. *Courtesy of Dale Ware Family Archives.*

Bobby Andresakis with crocodile.
*Courtesy of Krystal Knutson.*

Hal Newsom with cobra. *Courtesy of Hal Newsom*

Sea-Arama Marineworld

Skiers Starla Terry, Pam Pouncey, Ginny Bland. *Courtesy of Gin Thom.*

Wild Wet West Ski Show. *Courtesy of Gin Thom*

Skiers Dell Harkey, Starla Terry, Debbie McKinley. *Courtesy of Gin Thom.*

Skiers Starla Terry, Susan Minter Medford, Crystal Spangberg. *Courtesy of Gin Thom.*

Skiers Terry Moore, Wayne Esserman. *Courtesy of Gin Thom.*

Skier Ronnie Ginsberg without skis. *Courtesy of Gin Thom.*

Skiers Pam Pouncey (top), Ginny Bland (left), Starla Terry (right). *Courtesy of Gin Thom.*

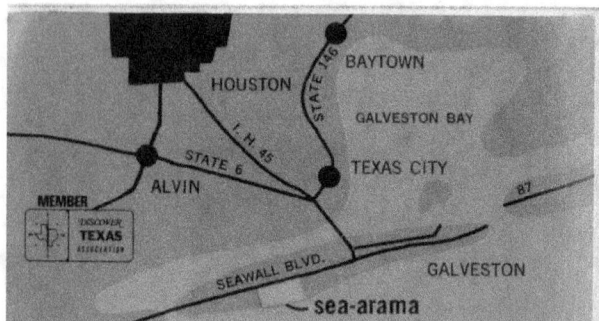

**LOCATION:** Sea-Arama Marineworld, on beautiful Galveston Island's West Beach is easily accessible by several major highways (see map). It is located at Seawall Boulevard and 91st Street, surrounded by the blue waters of the Gulf of Mexico and Galveston Bay. Large free parking area and only 45 minutes from Houston.

**BOX OFFICE HOURS:**
Open Daily, Year Round, 9 a.m. til dusk.

**FACILITIES:** Sea-Arama Marineworld is the warmth—the friendliness—the face of youth, hiring most of its staff from the ranks of college and high school students. It is beautifully landscaped and immaculately clean. Sea-Arama Marineworld is over 38-acres of great family fun and adventure. Sea-Arama is the world's most air-conditioned marine park and features covered stadiums for your comfort. We feature the **Treasure Chest** and **Tiki Gift Shops** with special gifts and treasures for your own memories and which make beautiful presents for your friends back home. And your family will love the **Pirate's Nook**, the highlight of our food facilities, surrounded by lush tropical gardens. We also have many different and varied food facilities throughout the park.
And don't forget your camera when you visit Sea-Arama Marineworld. We will assist you in obtaining wonderful pictures and have available complete facilities at the **Shutter Shop**.

**ADMISSION:** Adults (ages 13 and over) $3.50—Children (ages 3-12) $2.50—Children under 3 free with parent. One admission is all you pay to see all the shows and attractions at Sea-Arama Marineworld. Special prices for organized groups of 20 or more available. For information contact the Sales Department or Public Relations Department at the address below: *All prices and operating hours subject to change.*

Sea-Arama Marineworld Accepts:

Sea-Arama brochure. *Author's collection.*

## A MARINEWORLD OF FAMILY FUN

Sea-Arama Marineworld, a multi-million dollar marine attraction between the East & West coasts, offers you over four hours of unique family fun; featuring great shows . . . Mamuk, Sea-Arama's 5200 lb. Killer Whale, Marineworld Porpoise Revue, Noah's Ark (with Fat Albert the Elephant Seal, sea lions and penguins),

*S☆M☆A☆S☆H, a rollicking water ski comedy, Sea-Arama's Newest Attraction—A 108′ Two-Masted Schooner, the ''Southwind,'' Japanese Gardens and Bangladesh Sampan, Alligator Wrestling and Snake Show. Dive to the Deep Oceanarium Show, Seal and Sea Lion Feeding, Porpoise Petting Pool, Octopus Grotto, Tomb of the Lost Dolphin, Seven Seas Aquarium Tour and Garden of the Gods.

*This show is performed weekends only in Spring and daily in the Summer.

Sea-Arama brochure. *Author's collection.*

**Some of the employees:**

Adrianna Dubose Miller–Skier
Dr. A.J. Jinkins, MD–Employee doctor
Annye Davison–Mermaid
Augustine (Auggie) Almanza–Aquarium maintenance
Bryan Springer
Bobby Andresakis–Alligators, snakes
Bob Ford–Announcer
Bob Landers–Training director in August
Bryce Scherner–Skier
Anthony John (Bubba) Forester–skier
Clarence Pleasants–Director of landscaping
Crystal Spangberg–Skier
Debbie Lilly Autry–Skier
Debbie McKinley Williams–Skier
Dell Harkey–Skier
Dottie Carnes–Mermaid?
Ed Moore–Executive vice president and general manager
Ginny Bland–Skier
Greg Scofelia–Skier
Hal Jackson–Curator
Hal Newsom–Alligators, snakes, diver
James Watts–Food court manager
Jeff Brown–Skier
John Hill–Operations manager
Jim Ketcham–Alligator wrestler
Jim Parker–Trainer
Jimmie Sommerfield–Janitor, alligators, snakes
Jim Watts–Assistant operations manager
Joan Cole Wallace
John Braunsdorf–Skier
John Humason (Doc Rail)–Ski show director
Jon Littmann–Whale trainer, snake and alligator announcer
Ken Beggs–Trainer
Ken Gray–Curator/veterinarian

Ken Jones–Alligators, snakes
Kyle Janek–Skier
Luke Jordan–Snakes, alligators
Marie Long–Mermaid?
Mark Johnson–Skier
Mary Eggleston–Skier
Melissa McClellan–Mermaid, skier
Michelle Moore–Concessions, ticket booth, gift shop
Mike McNabb–Public Relations Director
Mike Pistone–Custodian, cook, food/beverage supervisor
Pam Pouncey–Skier
Pam Wilder–Ticket booth
Paula Trost–Mermaid '70–'72, Assistant curator for veterinarian
Perry Blackwell–Alligators, snakes, announcer
Ralph McPheeters?–Manager
Richard Biffle–Skier
Rhonda Ragone–Skier
Robert McClellan–Public relations manager
Ronnie Ginsberg–Skier
Sandy Boudreaux Scardino–Gift shop
Starla Terry–Skier
Steve Harris–Ski lead
Steve O'Donohoe–Director of live shows
Sue Johnson Flemke–Mermaid
Susan Minter Medford–Ski lead
Susie Ahern Knust–Whale Bar, Seahorse, Pirates Nook, Ski Hut, Pink Porpoise, Petting Zoo
Terry Moore–Ski show lead
Vaness Dudney Hamilton–Skier
Vernette Mathews Porter–Balloon girl, gift shop
Wayne Esserman–Skier
Wendy Fesler Millo–Gift shop

**Some of the Animals:**

Mother–porpoise
Lafitte–porpoise
Trace–porpoise
Lonesome–porpoise
Corky–porpoise
Ki-Ko–porpoise
Tiny Tina–porpoise
Squeaky–porpoise
Zippy–porpoise
Pebbles–porpoise

Lucy–porpoise
Sally–sea lion
Heidi–sea lion
Barnaby–seal
Kinook–seal
Kanuck–seal
Sea luck–seal
Mamuk–killer whale
Alligators
Snakes

# 1973

This year continued a terrible stretch of deaths at Sea-Arama that had started on October 21, 1972 and ran through January 1973. An outbreak of hepatitis, pneumonia, and other diseases killed fifteen porpoises. Soon after, Sea-Arama made a request to the federal government to import 10 porpoises, a second killer whale, and 20 sea lions.

Sea-Arama would sometimes send trainers and animals to local malls or events. On January 18, Luke Jordan was performing a Sea-Arama snake show at the boat show in Corpus Christi when he was struck by a cobra. He was sent to the local hospital and soon after made a complete recovery.

In February, the park announced that they would soon open the first section of their "Ships of the World" attraction. The schooner *Southwind* would be the centerpiece, while a portion of a Bangladesh sampan would be used as part of the entrance to the area. Later plans included re-outfitting *Southwind's* interior to be a floating museum of her history.

February was again scout month at Sea-Arama, when over 10,000 Boy Scouts, including cubs, explorers, scouts, and scout leaders, joined in Sea-Arama's annual salute to the scouts. 1973 was also a special year because it was the 63rd anniversary of the scouts.

A typical day for the scouts saw them arriving at 9 a.m. and receiving a Sea-Arama badge to be sewn on their Red Badge vest. They would wander around until 9:30 a.m., when the Seven Seas Tour started with the announcer describing the habits of each fish on display. A diver would feed the 200 different types of fish in the tank during the Dive to the Deep Show, and then in the mermaid/scuba show at 10:00 a.m., a mermaid swam around a skin diver demonstrating what would happen if he were shot with a spear gun. Luckily for the diver, the mermaid always came to his assistance with her air hose.

Later, at the Noah's Ark stadium, Noah's animals would do their tricks. A monkey would present a sign that read, "There's no business-like monkey business," a donkey would perform, a raccoon would turn his TV antenna to get better reception, and three penguins named Nixon, Agnew, and Johnson would do flips while diving into the water. Of course, the star of the show was Fat Albert, the elephant seal.

The next show they could see would be the alligator and snake show. The alligator would be rocked to sleep, walked around, and "burped" like a baby. During the snake part of the show, a trainer would work with venomous snakes such as pythons, rattlesnakes, and cobras.

The high point of the day for the boys would be when Mamuk the killer whale would jump out of the water to touch a ball suspended 25 feet in the air. Before the show ended, Mamuk would want to kiss a volunteer good-bye, and the volunteer would not only get a kiss but would also get soaked with water.

In 1973 Sea-Arama was selected to permanently house the record plaques for the Texas Saltwater Fishing Hall of Fame. The dedication was held on March 10. Beautiful eight-foot scrolls held the 39 bronze plaques that represented the 39 species of saltwater fish in Texas waters. When fish were caught that broke the record, they would be brought to Sea-Arama, where they would be mounted and displayed, along with the plaques and laminated walnut trophies that gave the record holders' info.

By May, *Southwind* had been completely refurbished on the outside.

This year's summer ski show was the new S.M.A.S.H theme.

By October it was becoming more and more difficult to find enough herring, because the Japanese were buying huge quantities of herring for use as food and fishery research. The shortage was affecting animals such as Mamuk, who ate 90 pounds of herring a day, and Fat Albert, who ate 30 pounds a day. In the past, Sea-Arama had gone through as much as 1,500 pounds of herring a day, but because of the shortage had started to use only 900 pounds a day. To try to solve the problem, the park started using more smelt because it was fairly easy to get.

In December eight alligators were released in a remote Texas coastal swamp because they had grown too old or too big to be kept at the park. They were later replaced with younger, smaller reptiles.

Alligators. *Courtesy of*
*www.windowtoaphotoworld.wordpress.com.*

S.M.A.S.H. ski show. *Courtesy of Gin Thom.*

Texas Saltwater Fishing Hall of Fame. *Courtesy of Dale Ware Family Archives.*

Trainer's head in the killer whale's mouth. *Courtesy Jovana Ivastanin.*

Ball jump during the Killer Whale Show. *Courtesy Jovana Ivastanin.*

Tim Gould

Volunteer time during the Killer Whale Show. *Courtesy Jovana Ivastanin.*

Killer Whale Show. *Courtesy Jovana Ivastanin.*

Killer Whale Show. *Courtesy of Jason Sullivan.*

Sea-Arama Marineworld

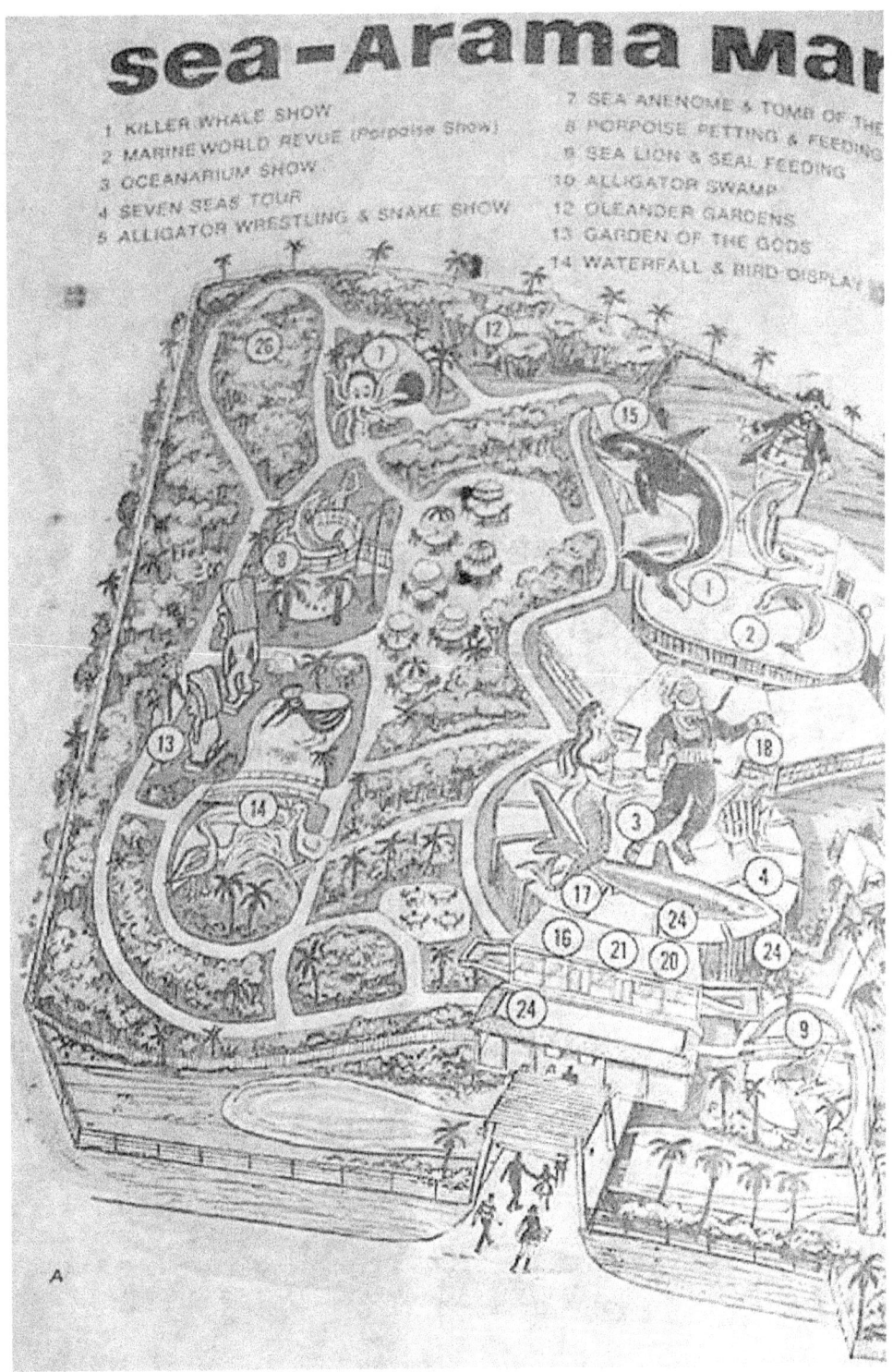

Sea-Arama map. *Courtesy of Donna at Mad Dogs Ranch.*

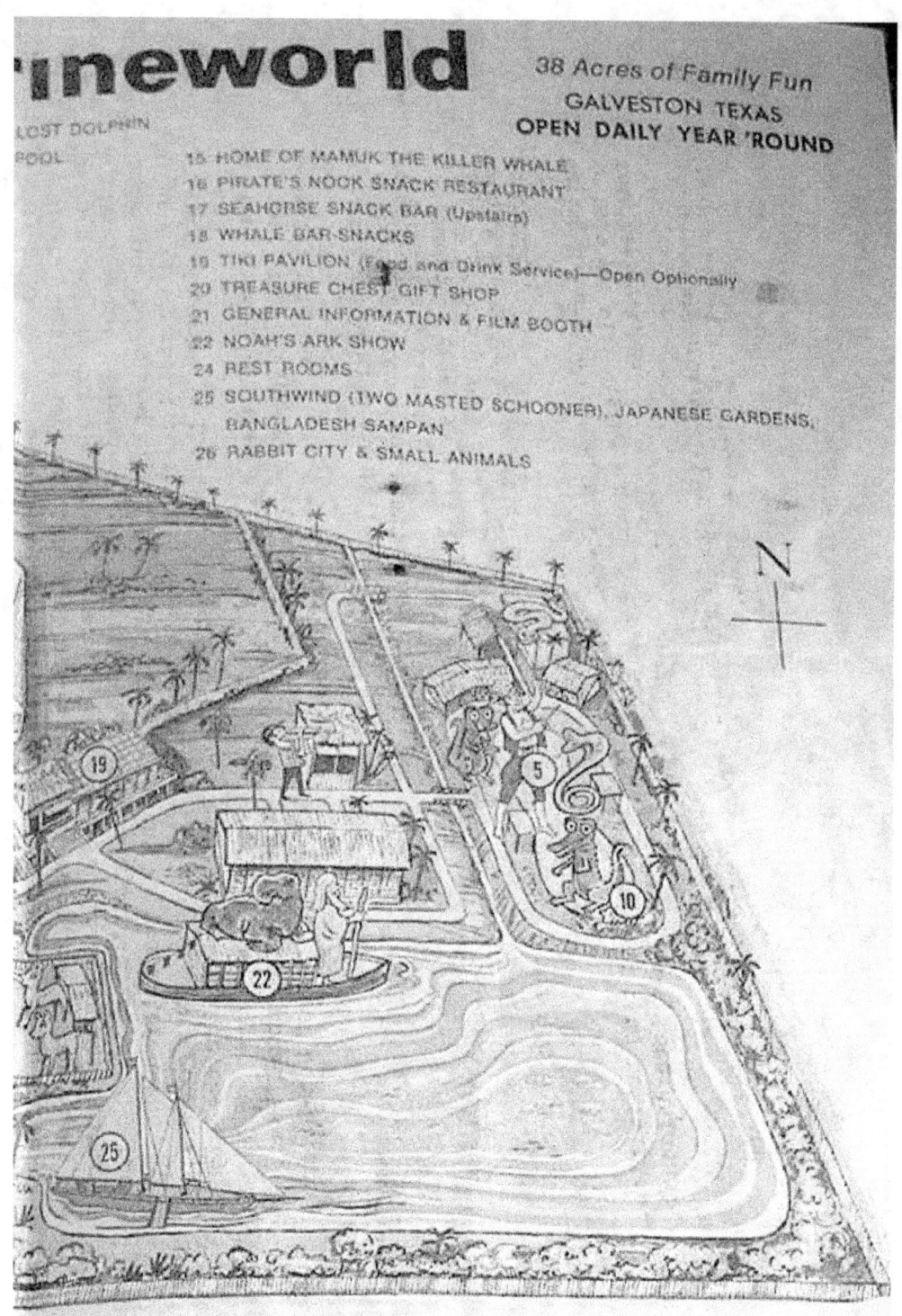

**rineworld**

38 Acres of Family Fun
GALVESTON TEXAS
OPEN DAILY YEAR 'ROUND

LOST DOLPHIN
POOL

15 HOME OF MAMUK THE KILLER WHALE
16 PIRATE'S NOCK SNACK RESTAURANT
17 SEAHORSE SNACK BAR (Upstairs)
18 WHALE BAR-SNACKS
19 TIKI PAVILION (Food and Drink Service)—Open Optionally
20 TREASURE CHEST GIFT SHOP
21 GENERAL INFORMATION & FILM BOOTH
22 NOAH'S ARK SHOW
24 REST ROOMS
25 SOUTHWIND (TWO MASTED SCHOONER), JAPANESE GARDENS,
   BANGLADESH SAMPAN
26 RABBIT CITY & SMALL ANIMALS

Sea-Arama map. *Courtesy of Donna at Mad Dogs Ranch.*

**Some of the employees:**
Adrianna Dubose Miller–Skier
Dr. A.J. Jinkins, MD–Employee doctor
Augustine (Auggie) Almanza–Aquarium maintenance
Bob Ford–Announcer
Bob Landers–Training director
Deek Vincent–Snakes, alligators
Dillard Bates–Snakes, alligators
Douglas Shimek–Trainer and assistant curator of animals
Ed Moore–Executive vice president and general manager
Edward (Stephen) Higgins–Assistant curator, night watchman, grounds helper
Fran Lloyd Galbreath–Group sales secretary
Fred Galbreath
Gayle Schreiber?–Trainer?
Hal Jackson–Curator
Hal Newsom–Alligators, snakes, diver
Helen Spangler Varner–Director of advertising and public relations
James Watts–Food court manager
Joan Cole Wallace
John Humason (Doc Rail)–Ski show director
Judy Zaun–Mermaid, trainer
Karen Eyvette Bankhead Guidry
Ken Beggs–Trainer

Ken Gray–Curator, veterinarian
Ken Jones–Alligators, snakes
Kyle Janek–Skier
Luke Jordan–Snakes, alligators
Marie Long–Mermaid?
Michelle Moore–Concessions, ticket booth, gift shop
Pam Wilder–Ticket booth
Paul Humason–Skier
Phillip Cowart–Kites, skier
Ralph McPheeters?–Manager
Rhonda Ragone–Skier
Ron Humason–Skier
Sandy Boudreaux Scardino–Gift shop
Steve Harris–Ski show manager
Steve O'Donohoe–Director of live shows
Susie Ahern Knust–Whale Bar, Seahorse, Pirates Nook, Ski Hut, Pink Porpoise, Petting Zoo
Terry Moore–Skier
Vaness Dudney Hamilton–Skier
Vernette Mathews Porter–Balloon girl, gift shop
Wendy Fesler Millo–Gift shop

**Some of the Animals:**
20 porpoises in June including:
Charlie Brown–porpoise
Mother–porpoise
Lafitte–porpoise
Trace–porpoise
Corky–porpoise
Connie–porpoise
Terry–porpoise
Lonesome–porpoise
Lucy–porpoise
Heidi–sea lion

Barnaby, Kinook–seal
Kanuck–seal
Fat Albert–elephant seal
Richard Nixon–penguin
Spiro Agnew, Johnson–penguin
Mamuk–killer whale
Deer/Donkey
Octopus/15 sharks
40 alligators
20 snakes
Pelicans/exotic birds

# 1974

The first half of 1974 was a busy time for Sea-Arama. The following would all occur within the first four months:

- A permit for adding another killer whale was being drafted.

- An announcement was made that *Southwind's* interior would be worked on; she would either become a maritime museum or have musicals performed on her deck.

- The Boy Scouts would be attending a choral festival in April.

- There would be a band festival in March.

- The Baptist youth festival would occur in July.

- In May would be the second Annual Gulf Coast International Folk Festival.

- April would bring a science day at the park.

- Sea-Arama would be participating in scientific research programs with the University of Texas medical branch, the Marine Biomedical Institute, and Texas A&M University Maritime Academy.

The Folklife Festival in May and June lasted two weeks and was a big hit. Beside the regularly scheduled shows, visitors could hear "Polish, Calypso and Oriental Dancers, Mexican Mariachis, jazz ballet, Scottish pipe & drums and folk songs from around the world." They could also enjoy food and drink from countries like Mexico, Jamaica, Italy, Ireland, and Germany.

Sea-Arama Marineworld

June Show Schedule:

|  |  |
|------|------|
| 9:00 | Park Opens |
| 9:10 | Seven Seas Tour |
| 9:30 | Oceanarium Show |
| 10:00 | Noah's Ark Show |
| 10:30 | Alligator Wrestling/Snake Show |
| 11:00 | Water Ski Comedy |
| 11:40 | Marine Animal Training Workshop |
| 12:05 | Marineworld Revue (Porpoise Show) |
| 12:35 | Porpoise Feeding |
| 12:55 | Intermission |
| 1:25 | Oceanarium Show or Water Ski Comedy |
| 2:05 | Alligator Wrestling/Snake Show or Porpoise Show |
| 2:40 | Noah's Ark Show |
| 3:20 | Water Ski Comedy |
| 4:00 | Marine Animal Training Workshop |
| 4:30 | Marineworld Revue (Porpoise Show) or Alligator Wrestling/Snake Show |
| 5:00 | Seal Feeding |
| 5:25 | Oceanarium Show |
| 6:00 | Noah's Ark Show |
| 6:30 | Alligator Wrestling/Snake Show |
| 7:00 | Water Ski Comedy |
| 7:40 | Marineworld Revue (Porpoise Show) |
| 8:10 | Oceanarium Show |
| 8:30 | Park Closes |

Everything looked positive at Sea-Arama until tragedy struck on June 14: Mamuk died. Autopsy reports said he died of asphyxiation or acute streptococcal septicemia. He was approximately ten and a half years old. Officials didn't know how the death occurred, but they ruled out drowning, vandalism, inadequacies in food, and water quality. He had been their main attraction and greatly loved by the staff and public.

Sea-Arama knew they needed another whale as soon as possible, so the word was sent out. A new whale was expected to arrive within two weeks.

August 17 was Ragin' Cajun Day, with featured singer Doug Kershaw, who sang the popular song, "Louisiana Man." Comedian Justin Wilson appeared with him, and the public enjoyed a variety of Cajun foods, including jambalaya, gumbo, shrimp pie, red beans, and rice.

Hal Newsom "Kiss of Death" during the
Alligator Wrestling/Snake Show. *Courtesy of Greg May.*

Porpoise Show with Jennifer Varner as volunteer.
*Courtesy of Helen Varner.*

Hal Newsom in the Alligator Wrestling Show. *Courtesy of Hal Newsom.*

**Some of the employees:**
Alice Law–Public relations, front gate supervisor, assistant accountant
Dr. A.J. Jinkins, MD–Employee doctor
Augustine (Auggie) Almanza–Aquarium maintenance
Bob Ford–Announcer
Bruce Staples–Skier
Dave Richtman–Curator and general animal trainer
Douglas Shimek–Trainer and assistant curator of animals
Ed Moore–Executive vice president and general manager
Edward (Stephen) Higgins–Assistant curator, night watchman, grounds help
Hal Jackson–Curator
Hal Newsom–Alligators, snakes, diver
Helen Spangler Varner–Director of advertising and public relations

James Watts–Food court manager
Joan Cole Wallace
John Humason (Doc Rail)–Ski show director
Judy Zaun–Trainer
Karen Eyvette Bankhead Guidry
Ken Beggs–Director of training
Ken Gray–Curator, veterinarian
Ken Jones–Alligators, snakes
Kyle Janek–Skier
Michelle Moore–Concessions, ticket booth, gift shop
Pam Apffel DelPapa–Skier
Pat Apffel Whittington–Skier
Paul Humason–Skier
Steve O'Donohoe–Director of live shows
Terry Moore–Skier
Vernette Mathews Porter–Balloon girl, gift shop

**Some of the Animals:**
Eight porpoises added to equal twenty
Charlie Brown–porpoise
Mother–porpoise
Zsa-Zsa–porpoise
Lafitte–porpoise
Trace–porpoise
Sam–porpoise
Connie–porpoise
Terry–porpoise
Lonesome–porpoise
Corky–porpoise
Lucy–porpoise
Mamuk–killer whale
Tuna–sea lion

Sandy–sea lion
Constance–sea lion
Heidi–sea lion
Barnaby–seal
Kinook–seal
Kanuck–seal
Fat Albert–elephant seal
Over 500 fish
Deer
Donkey
40 alligators
20 snakes
15 sharks
Various exotic birds
Turtles
Crabs
Cobra

# 1975

On May 27 Sea-Arama welcomed its new $35,000 whale, flown to Galveston from California. Tiffany was a young, 13-foot-long female pilot whale. She weighed about 1,200 pounds and was expected to attain a length of 16 feet and weigh 2,000 pounds at maturity. The whale was captured by Marineland of the Pacific and went through a period of isolation to check her health and to give her an opportunity to adjust before being flown to Texas.

The whale was placed on public display soon after arriving at Sea-Arama and began training for her own show as soon as she adjusted to her surroundings. The plan was to do all the training sessions in view of the public to give people an opportunity to observe what was involved in preparing an animal for a show. But all the park's plans did not work out as they hoped.

Almost exactly a year after Mamuk died, Tiffany, the new pilot whale, died on the morning of June 13. The cause of death was not immediately determined.

In 1975, Sea-Arama began transitioning to contracting with companies to provide all of its shows.

The porpoise show stadium was re-designed around 1975 so that there was a stage that could be raised and lowered by a winch for the sea lions to perform their show.

In June Sea-Arama was advertising the newest animal additions to the park: Himalayan black bears. They would be performing in a new show soon, but in the meantime, visitors could enjoy watching the bears, along with other animals like raccoons and kangaroos, while they were trained.

In September Sea-Arama was busy advertising the schooner *Southwind*, the shark and mermaid show, porpoise feeding, the three bears training sessions, penguins, the snake show, the alligator show, and a swimming pig and kangaroo that played a music box in the Noah's Ark show.

Himalayan black bear. *Courtesy of Dale Ware Family Archives.*

Tower fish jump. *Courtesy of Krystal Knutson*

Porpoise bows. *Courtesy of Krystal Knutson.*

Ken Beggs and Tiffany the pilot whale (with white zinc oxide on her skin). *Author's collection.*

Ken Jones holding alligator's mouth open. *Courtesy of Krystal Knutson.*

Sea-Arama Marineworld

Sea-Arama map. *Author's collection.*

Sea-Arama map. *Author's collection.*

**Some of the employees:**
Alice Law–Public Relations, Front gate supervisor, assistant accountant
Dr. A.J. Jinkins, MD–Employee doctor
Augustine (Auggie) Almanza–Aquarium maintenance
Bob Ford–Announcer
Brandy Smith–Assistant curator and trainer of marine mammals, bird shows, underwater choreography
Bruce Staples–Ski show
Dale Ware–General manager
Dave Richtman–Curator, general animal trainer, bear show
Douglas Shimek–Trainer and assistant curator of animals
Ed Moore–Executive vice president and general manager
Edward (Stephen) Higgins–Assistant curator, night watchman, grounds help
Greg Samford–Janitor, landscaping, maintenance
Hal Jackson–Curator
Hal Newsom–Alligators, snakes, diver
Helen Spangler Varner–Director of advertising and public relations
James Watts–Food court manager

Joan Cole Wallace
John Humason (Doc Rail)–Ski show director
Judith Buff–Administrative assistant in public relations
Judy Zaun–Trainer
Karen Eyvette Bankhead Guidry
Kelly Carnes Johns–Ticket booth, greeter
Ken Beggs–Director of training
Ken Gray–Curator, veterinarian
Ken Jones–Alligator, snakes
Kyle Janek–Skier
Linda Eliason–Concessions
Michelle Moore–Concessions, ticket booth, gift shop
Pam Apffel DelPapa–Skier
Pat Apffel Whittington–Skier
Paul Humason–Skier
Paul Ware–Trash pickup and fish sales at sea lion and porpoise petting pools
Ron Pittman–Assistant director of training
Stacy Jones–Mermaid
Steve O'Donohoe–Director of live shows
Terry Moore–Skier
Vernette Mathews Porter–Balloon girl, gift shop

**Some of the Animals:**
Leaperace–kangaroo
Wallabies
Bears (Bruizer was one of four Himalayan black bears in Dec '75)
Raccoons
Penguins
Pig
Tiffany–pilot whale
Charlie Brown–porpoise
Lafitte–porpoise
Zsa-Zsa–porpoise

Connie, Terry, Beta–porpoise
Alpha, Sigma, Gamma–porpoise
Lonesome, Trace, Shadow–porpoise
Key, Lucy–porpoise
Tuna, Duffer, Sandy- sea lion
Aramis, Constance, Heidi–sea lion
Jill–sea lion
Barnaby, Kinook, Whitie–seal
Blackie–seal
Poncho–elephant seal

# 1976

In 1976 the new bear show premiered. The park advertised it in all the local newspapers as a "favorite fable brought to life by the Sea-Arama performers; Goldilocks and the Three Bears."

Other shows this year included the Oceanarium (Dive to the Deep Show), Shark-Mermaid Show, Seven Seas Tour, Porpoise Revue, Noah's Ark, Snake and Alligator Show, and the spring and summer ski shows. The new shows premiering this year were the Exotic Bird Show, the Three Bears Show, and the Southwind Musical Variety Show.

This year Sea-Arama began contracting with the company Entertainment Plus to provide narration and show production for Sea-Arama's shows.

Sea-Arama also began this year to contract with the company Ocean Action to provide the porpoise and sea lion shows.

In April Sea-Arama began promoting a contest asking the public to submit names for the new costumed characters. These goodwill ambassadors would include Tulip the dancing bear and Buttons the dancing dolphin.

In June "A Salute to Man and the Sea" debuted on *Southwind's* deck. The piano player for the musical was David Little, who also performed with Kathy Incaprera (guitar) several times a day in the Garden of the Gods area.

Also in June the bird show began to be performed as its own show in the alligator and snake arena rather than as part of the Noah's Ark Show in the Ski Stadium.

*Free Petting Given Here*

Petting Zoo. *Author's collection.*

Sea-Arama shows are on continuously. Dine in the snack bar or enjoy the picnic areas in tropical gardens. See the exotic bird display, Tomb of the Lost Dolphin, Pirate's Cove Pub.

Aerial photo of Sea-Arama. Alligator/snake arena in bottom center, ski show stadium directly above it. Oceanarium directly above ski show stadium. Porpoise stadium to the right of the Oceanarium. *Author's collection.*

Hal Newsom during Alligator Wrestling/Snake Show. *Courtesy of Hal Newsom.*

Hal Newsom during Alligator Wrestling/Snake Show. *Courtesy of Hal Newsom.*

Costumed characters Tulip and Buttons.
*Photo by Stan Begam, courtesy of Greg May.*

*Romantic Southwind Schooner*

*Southwind* at Sea-Arama. *Author's collection.*

Sea-Arama Marineworld

Sea-Arama brochure. *Author's collection.*

**Some of the employees:**

Alice Law–Public relations, front gate supervisor, assistant accountant
Dr. A.J. Jinkins, MD–Employee doctor
Augustine (Auggie) Almanza–Aquarium maintenance
Bob Ford–Announcer
Brandy Smith–Assistant curator and trainer of marine mammals, bird shows, underwater choreography
Bruce Staples–Skier
Craig Janek–Skier
Dale Ware–General manager
David Harris
Dave Richtman–Curator, general animal trainer, bear show
David Shinn–Curator in seal grotto
Debby O'Connor Chambers–Administrative assistant to general manager, guest relations
Diana Edwards–Concessions
Douglas Shimek–Trainer and assistant curator of animals
Edward (Stephen) Higgins–Assistant curator, night watchman, grounds help
Ellen Lindsay–Petting zoo
Gene Ogle–Assistant snake handler
Greg Samford–Janitor, landscaping, Maint.
Hal Newsom–Alligators, snakes, diver
Helen Spangler Varner–Advertising/P.R.
James Watts–Food court manager
Joan Cole Wallace
John Humason (Doc Rail)–Ski show director

Judith Buff–Administrative assistant in public relations
Judy Zaun–Trainer
Karen Eyvette Bankhead Guidry
Kelly Carnes Johns–Ticket booth, greeter
Ken Beggs–Dir of training, curator of animals
Ken Jones–Snakes
Ken Ramirez–Announcer
Kyle Janek–Skier
Mary Jo Urbani–Skier
Mike Sass–Trainer of bears, sea lions, dolphins
Pam Apffel DelPapa–Skier
Pat Apffel Whittington–Skier
Paul Cotter–Janitor
Paul Ware–Fish sales at sea lion and porpoise petting pools
Paul Humason–Skier
Ralph McPheeters–Manager
Richard (Ritchie) Nunez–Trainer
Sharon McMahon Enge–Mermaid
Stacy Jones–Mermaid
Steve O'Donohoe–Director of live shows
Stephen Pulley–Front gate, skier
Susan Kamps–Mermaid, bird show
Terry Moore–Skier
Tim Bernsen–Handing out maps, porpoise petting pool, assistant curator, buttons the dancing dolphin
Valentine Alfaro Flores–Concessions stand upstairs and down

**Some of the Animals:**

Leaperace–kangaroo
Harpo–gibbon ape
Charlie Brown, Zsa Zsa–porpoise
Connie, Terry, Beta–porpoise
Alpha, Sigma, Gamma–porpoise
Lonesome, Key, Lucy–porpoise

Tuna, Duffer, Sandy–sea lion
Aramis, Constance, Jill–sea lion
Barnaby, Kinook, Houdini–seal
Whitie, Blackie–seal
Poncho–elephant seal
Exotic birds
Himalayan black bears

# 1977

This year Sea-Arama proudly proclaimed that it was unique: it was the only marine-oriented entertainment park open daily all year long between the east and west coasts, and it offered more continuous shows and attractions (25) than any other marine park in the country.

Some of the shows and attractions included:

- Porpoise Revue
- Sea Lion Show
- Oceanarium Mermaid Show called "Alice in Waterland"
- Himalayan Black Bears Show
- Tropical Bird Show
- M.A.T.W. (Marine Animal Training Workshop)
- Exhibit of alligators
- Exhibit of piranha
- Exhibit of sharks
- Exhibit of turtles
- Exhibit of Brown pelicans
- Reptile/Snake Show
- Southwind Musical Variety Show (during the summer)

- Water Ski Show–S.M.A.S.H (during the summer)
- Seven Seas Tour
- Puppet Show
- Dive to the Deep Show
- Tulip and Buttons Show (costumed characters)

There were some new shows this year including the Tulip and Buttons show. These two costumed characters and an ill-mannered pirate performed on the schooner *Southwind*, where children booed the pirate and encouraged Tulip and Buttons to protect the *Southwind* treasure.

Another new show that started in June was the "Alice in Waterland" show. The theme followed Alice's adventures into the undersea world and her efforts to return to life on the surface. It included mermaids and more than 250 kinds of gulf fish that were in the Oceanarium.

Additionally, there was a new puppet show.

The park no longer had a combination alligator and snake show. The alligators were now on display with the snake show being renamed as the Reptile Show.

In 1977 the staff of Sea-Arama attempted to save Pilgrim, a pygmy sperm whale that had been beached on the Galveston shores and received much media attention. He ultimately did not survive.

A porpoise was accidentally captured in June in a fisherman's net and brought to Sea-Arama to receive treatment. At five or six years old, "Lucky" ultimately survived his injuries and later became the mascot for Sea-Arama and the Marine Mammal Stranding Network.

In October Sea-Arama began offering elementary kids behind-the-scenes tours. With more than 15,000 school children visiting the park each year, the response was overwhelming, and the program had to be shut down. Instead, the park created an educational program that went to the schools. But it too had an overwhelming response and had to be discontinued. In the end, the park created a slide show presentation that schools could borrow.

Pam Apffel, Pat Apffel, Ruthie Parker Kelly?
*Author's collection.*

Skiers Paul (Rail) Humason, Jane Anne Rogers Jordan, Kimberly Allen, and Bill Ansell. *Courtesy of Lisa Glaves Merrow.*

Hal Newsom with volunteers and announcer Steve O'Donohoe. *Courtesy of Helen Varner.*

Barrel-Walking Himalayan Black Bear

Three bears show. *Author's collection.*

Hurdle Leaping California Sea Lion

Sea lion show. *Author's collection.*

**Some of the employees:**

Alice Law–Public relations, front gate supervisor, assistant accountant

Dr. A.J. Jinkins, MD–Employee doctor

Augustine (Auggie) Almanza–Aquarium maintenance

Bill Ansell–Skier

Bob Ford–Announcer

Brandy Smith–Assistant curator and trainer of marine mammals, bird shows, underwater choreography

Bruce Staples–Skier

Craig Janek–Skier

Dale Ware–General manager

David Shinn–Curator in seal grotto

Debby Chambers–Administrative assistant to general manager, guest relations

Debbie Murray–Secretary to the G.M.

Donna Johnson Smith–Mermaid, bird shows, animal costumes

Douglas Shimek–Trainer and assistant curator of animals

Frank Crawley?–Puppets

Greg Samford–Janitor, landscaping, maintenance

Hal Newsom–Director of reptiles

Helen Spangler Varner–Director of advertising and public relations

James Watts–Food court manager

John Humason (Doc Rail)–Ski show director

Judy Zaun–Trainer

Kelly Carnes Johns–Ticket booth, greeter

Ken Beggs–Director of training, curator of animals

Ken Ramirez–Announcer, trainer

Kevin Colston–Snakes

Kevin W. Mullet–Parking attendant, photographer

Kimberly Allen–Skier

Margaret Almanza Cuellar–Concessions

Mary Jo Urbani–Skier

Mike Sass–Trainer of bears, sea lions, dolphins

Nick O'Donohoe–Food service

Pam Apffel DelPapa–Skier

Pat Apffel Whittington–Skier

Paul Cotter–Janitor

Paul Ware–Curator

Paul (Rail) Humason–Skier

Ralph McPheeters–Manager

Richard Burns

Richard Nunez–Trainer

Robin Rader–Snake handler

Russell O'Connor–Director of maintenance/operations

Ruthie Parker Kelly–Skier

Sharon McMahon Enge–Mermaid

Stephen Pulley–Front gate, skier

Steve O'Donohoe–Director of live shows

Susan Kamps–Mermaid, bird show

Tami Dodson–Skier, petting zoo, parking lot, bird show

Terry Moore–Skier

Tim Bernsen–Handing out maps, porpoise petting pool, assistant curator, Buttons the dancing dolphin

Valentine Alfaro Flores–Concession stands

**Some of the Animals:**

Himalayan black bears

Cuddles–boa constrictor

Charlie Brown, Zsa Zsa, Lucky–porpoise

Connie, Terry, Beta–porpoise

Alpha, Sigma, Key, Lucy–porpoise

Tuna, Duffer, Sandy, Aramis–sea lion

Constance, Jill–sea lion

Barnaby–seal

Houdini–seal

Whitie–seal

Blackie–seal

Exotic birds

Alligators

Snakes

# 1978

The big news for 1978 was the new show that premiered in November, "Jungle Fantasy Wild Cat Show."

On July 4th the Aqua Thrill Way opened next to Sea-Arama on the seawall boulevard, where there is now (in 2016) a miniature golf course.

Craig Caskey with cobra. *Courtesy of Craig Caskey.*

John Campolongo. *Author's collection.*

Hoop of fire jump with trainer Haste Harold.
*Courtesy of Craig Caskey.*

Sea-Arama brochure. *Author's collection.*

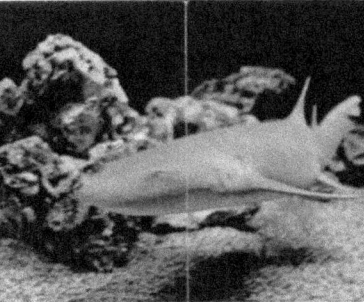

# The Gulf Coast's great sea life park is . . .

## sea-Arama
## marineworld

Beautiful, bright, awe inspring creatures from oceans the world over. Performing for you. Alive and kicking in an environment scientifically designed to make them feel at home. Atlantic Bottle-Nosed Dolphins and California Sea Lions headline their own celebrated revues. You can even see how Sea-Arama conducts school for its new recruits in the fascinating Marine Animal Training Workshops.

Take the remarkable Seven Seas Tour for a close up look at hundreds of rare aquatic species. Each beautifully lighted aquarium is a model of its inhabitant's home waters. The center stage attraction on the Seven Seas Tour is our 160,000 gallon salt water oceanarium. Huge plate glass windows reveal monster size sharks, stingarees, groupers, gar, turtles and more.

And if you happen to be wondering what it would be like to be inside the oceanarium with those big guys, stick around for the Dive to the Deep show. See a diver descend into the oceanarium and feed those giants by hand. You'll hear him through a special microphone inside his helmet.

Sea-Arama Marineworld also features shows and attractions in addition to those dealing with marinelife. The unforgettable Snake Show is unmatched in the nation. Deadly King Cobras, Burmese Pythons and Texas Rattle Snakes are the headliners. Hold your breath while the Sea-Arama reptile handler actually kisses a Cobra on top of its raised hood!

While at Sea-Arama Marineworld be sure to meet Ali Macaw and Harvey in the Tropical Bird Show. See South American Scarlet and Green Macaws and Cockatoos perform on roller skates and other surprises.

A favorite with children is the small animal petting zoo and be sure to see the Brown Pelican exhibit. Through coordination with the Texas Department of Parks and Wildlife and the U.S. Department of the Interior Fish and Wildlife Service, Sea-Arama is attempting to reestablish the endangered Brown Pelican species along the Gulf Coast.

Sea-Arama brochure. *Author's collection.*

**Some of the employees:**

Alice Law–Public relations, front gate supervisor, assistant accountant
Amber Jinkins Shelley–Birds
Augustine (Auggie) Almanza–Aquarium maintenance
Dr. A.J. Jinkins, MD–Employee doctor
Bob Ford–Announcer
Brandy Smith–Assistant curator & trainer of marine mammals, bird shows, underwater choreography
Craig Caskey–Snakes
Craig Janek–Skier
Bruce Staples–Skier
Dale Ware–General manager
David Flores–Food concessions
David Schaper
Debby Chambers–Administrative assistant to general manager, guest relations
Donna Johnson Smith–Mermaid, bird shows, animal costumes
Elia Limon
Frank Cardenas–Director of special projects
Greg Samford–Janitor, landscaping, maintenance
Haste Harold–Skier, trainer
James Watts–Food court manager
John Campolongo–Big cat show
John Humason (Doc Rail)–Ski show owner
John Kerivan–Head curator of animal health and husbandry
Johnny Carter–Ski manager
Judy Zaun–Trainer
Karen Van Etten–Gift shop, food services

Ken Beggs–Director of training, curator of animals
Ken Ramirez–Announcer, trainer
Kent Dodge–Skier
Lewis Densman
Mary Jo Urbani–Skier
Mike Schultz–Trainer dolphins, sea lions
Mike Sass–Trainer of bears, sea lions, dolphins
Nick O'Donohoe–Skier
Pam Apffel DelPapa–Skier
Pat Apffel Whittington–Skier
Paul Ware–Trainer, dolphin, sea lion shows
Paul Humason–Skier
Richard Burns
Richard Nunez–Trainer
Robin Rose–Gift shop/shell shop employee and cashier
Russell O'Connor–Director of maintenance/operations
Russ Ware–Skier
Sharon Little Campolongo–Big cat show, concessions
Sharon McMahon Enge–Mermaid
Steve O'Donohoe–Director of live shows
Susan Kamps–Mermaid, bird show
Tami Dodson–Skier, petting zoo, parking lot, bird show
Terry Moore–Skier
Valentine Alfaro Flores–Concession stands upstairs and down
Victor Sorrento–Snake handler, curator, maintenance, announcer, marine mammal trainer

**Some of the Animals:**

Charlie Brown, Zsa Zsa, Lucky–dolphin
Connie, Terry, Beta, Key–dolphin
Sigma, Alpha, Big Al, Lucy–dolphin
Tuna, Duffer, Sandy–sea lion
Aramis, Constance–sea lion

Barnaby, Whitie, Blackie–seal
Ravi–Bengal tiger
Sabra–Asian leopard
Kunta–black panther
Duke–German shepherd dog

# 1979

By 1979, Sea-Arama was announcing that it was a successful business venture that had shown a profit every year since it opened.

At the end of February, the curating department installed a 400-gallon aquarium that housed a community of smaller fish that couldn't be displayed with the larger ones. During this era, the curating department in the Oceanarium had both a library and a laboratory.

February 25 was the last mention of the schooner *Southwind* in print in the Galveston Daily News, when Sea-Arama announced that plans were in the works to isolate the schooner and "create an atmosphere by narration and musical background that would allow visitors to relax and envision the romantic days of the schooner."

This year's shows included the Disco Dolphin Revue, Sea Lion Water Olympics, Venomous Snake Handling/Reptile Show, Exotic Bird Pirate Frolics, Oceanarium Deep Sea Diver Show, Jungle Fantasy Wild Cat Show, and summer Ski Show.

There were some changes this year: the small animal petting zoo was removed, and a children's playground was built in its place. Also, all major exhibits at Sea-Arama were now being narrated by tape recording. The landscaping included a special section to display plants indigenous to the Gulf Coast, and finally, thousands of dollars had been spent in new and improved sound equipment for the park, with a new communication system installed in the ticket booth.

John Campolongo and the Jungle Fantasy Wild Cat Show. *Courtesy of Greg May.*

C. Michael Bailey, Leonard the lion, and trainer Richard Nunez on the right. *Courtesy of Lisa Glaves Merrow.*

Paul Ware with Jones the sea lion. *Courtesy of Dale Ware Family Archives.*

**sea-arama marineworld**

Galveston Island, Texas
50 Miles South of Houston
Open every day of the year!

Sea-Arama Marineworld opens daily at 10 a.m . All shows and attractions operate consecutively every day until dark. Major credit cards are accepted.

Special rates are available to groups of 15 or more. Contact Marketing Department, Sea-Arama Marineworld. P. O. Box 3068, Galveston, Texas 77553 or call (713) 744-4501. From Houston: 488-4441.

All prices, shows and operating hours are subject to change.

**ALIVE WITH EXCITEMENT!**

**sea-Arama marineworld**

West Beach / Seawall Blvd. & 91st
Galveston Island, Texas

Sea-Arama brochure. *Author's collection.*

Tim Gould

# The Gulf Coast's great sea life park is . . .

Sea-Arama Marineworld is a delightful and educational experience for all ages. Its lush tropical landscaping covers 38 acres. Plan to spend a few hours or come for the whole day. In either event you'll find Sea-Arama Marineworld a worthwhile experience. It's a great entertainment value!

# ALIVE WITH EXCITEMENT!

Sea-Arama brochure. *Author's collection.*

# The Gulf Coast's great sea life park is . . .

## sea-arama marineworld

Beautiful, bright, awe-inspiring creatures from oceans the world over. Performing for you. Alive and kicking in an environment scientifically designed to make them feel at home. Dazzling performances by Atlantic Bottle-Nosed Dolphins and California Sea Lions headline Sea-Arama's entertainment package. You'll even see how Sea-Arama conducts school for its new recruits in

the fascinating Marine Animal Training Workshops.

Take the remarkable Seven Seas Tour for a close-up look at hundreds of rare aquatic species. Each beautifully lighted aquarium is a model of its inhabitant's home waters. The center stage attraction of the Seven Seas Tour is our 160,000 gallon salt water oceanarium. Huge plate glass windows reveal monster-size sharks,

stingarees, groupers, gar, turtles and more. See a diver feed them by hand!

Sea-Arama Marineworld also features shows and attractions in addition to those dealing with marinelife. See our fearless, wild animal trainer orchestrate the new Jungle Fantasy Show. Accompan-

ied only by his faithful German Shepherd, he performs with snarling adversaries, including a huge Bengal Tiger, spotted leopard and a black panther.

"Almost Anything Goes" in the precision high jinks of our comedy water ski show during the spring and summer months.

Sea-Arama's unforgettable Snake Show is unmatched in the

nation. Deadly King Cobras, Burmese Pythons and Texas Rattle Snakes are the headliners.

Meet Ali Macaw and Harvey in the Tropical Bird Show. See South American Scarlet and Green Macaws and Cockatoos

roller skate and perform other surprising feats.

A favorite with children is the fun-filled "Big Toy" playground. It's full of things to swing on, climb over and slide down.

Sea-Arama has several concession areas offering plenty of good things to eat and drink. Or if you prefer, pack a lunch and enjoy our shaded picnic area. Group rates and company or organization picnics can be arranged and catered for groups of 15 or more. Contact the Sea-Arama Marketing Department for more information, (713) 744-4501.

Sea-Arama brochure. *Author's collection.*

**Some of the employees:**

Alice Law–Public Relations, Front gate supervisor, assistant accountant
Amber Jinkins Shelley–Birds
Augustine (Auggie) Almanza–Aquarium maintenance
Dr. A.J. Jinkins, MD–Employee doctor
Barry Proctor
Bob Ford–Announcer
Brandy Smith–Assistant curator, trainer of marine mammals, birds, underwater choreography
Bruce Staples–Skier
C. Michael Bailey–Assistant curator
Craig Janek–Skier
Dale Ware–General manager
Debby Chambers–Administrative assistant to general manager, guest relations
Donna Johnson Smith–Mermaid, bird shows, animal costumes
Greg Samford–Janitor, landscaping, maintenance
James Watts–Food court manager
John Kerivan–Head curator of animal health and husbandry
John Campolongo–Big cat show
Judy Proctor Sanders–The Nook
Judy Zaun–Trainer
Karen Van Etten–Gift shop, food services
Ken Beggs–Director of training, curator of animals
Ken Ramirez–Announcer, trainer
Kent Dodge–Skier
Kim Piel Conner–Skier

Linda Meyer Sivy–Snack bar, skier
Mary Jo Urbani–Skier
Mike Cromie–Pirates Nook snack bar, supervisor of food services, groundskeeper supervisor
Mike Sass–Trainer of bears, sea lions, dolphins
Mike Schultz–Trainer dolphins, sea lions
Nick O'Donohoe–Skier
Pam Apffel DelPapa–Skier
Pat Apffel Whittington–Skier
Paul Ware–Trainer, dolphins, sea lions
Paul Humason–Skier
Richard Nunez–Trainer
Richard Burns
Russell O'Connor–Director of maintenance/operations
Russ Ware–Skier
Sharon Little Campolongo–Big cats, concessions
Sharon McMahon Enge–Mermaid
Steve O'Donohoe–Director of live shows
Susan Kamps–Mermaid, bird show
Tammy Crow
Tami Dodson–Skier, petting zoo, parking lot, bird show
Terry Moore–Ski show director
Terry Overstreet–Live show director and announcer
Victor Sorrento–Snake handler, curator, maintenance, announcer, marine mammal trainer

**Some of the Animals:**

Charlie Brown, Zsa Zsa, Lucky–dolphin
Connie, Hastings, Lucy–dolphin
Terry, Beta, Alpha–dolphin
Sigma, Big Al–dolphin
Tuna, Duffer, Sandy–sea lion

Aramis, Constance–sea lion
Barnaby, Whitie, Blackie–seal
Ravi–Bengal tiger
Sabra–Asian leopard
Kunta–black panther
Duke–German shepherd dog
Leonard–lion

# 1980

By 1980, Sea-Arama's attendance numbers were impressive for a small park, with an average annual attendance of 305,000. In the fifteen years it had been open, more than 4,275,000 paid guests had come through its doors. This year the park was announcing that it had the largest number of different shows of any sea-life park in the U.S.

The Jungle Fantasy Wild Cat Show was still going strong in 1980, with three shows a day. In April, Ivan, a 17-month-old Siberian tiger, arrived in Galveston from the Utica Zoo in New York to become part of the show.

Kevin Patton with lions Dante and Timba. *Courtesy of Kevin Patton.*

Jungle Fantasy Wild Cat Show. *Courtesy of Hal Newsom.*

**Some of the employees:**

Alice Law–Public relations, front gate supervisor, assistant accountant

Amber Jinkins Shelley–Birds

Dr. A.J. Jinkins, MD–Employee doctor

Augustine (Auggie) Almanza–Aquarium maintenance

Becky Russell–Janitor, food service cashier

Bob Ford–Announcer

Bruce Staples–Skier

Craig Janek–Skier

Dale Ware–General manager/president of Sea-Arama Corporation in February

Debby Chambers–Administrative assistant to general manager, guest relations

Donna Johnson Smith–Mermaid, bird shows, animal costumes

Gene Lucas–Vice president of organization

Greg Samford–Janitor, landscaping, maintenance

Jack Dismukes–Chairman of the board

John Boysen–Concessions at Pirates Nook

John Kerivan–Head curator of animal health and husbandry

John Campolongo–Big cat show

Karen Van Etten–Gift shop, food services

Kelley Grush–Announcer, bird trainer, dolphin training

Ken Beggs–Director of training, curator of animals

Ken Ramirez–Announcer, trainer

Kent Dodge–Skier

Kevin Patton–Big cat show

Kim Piel Conner–Skier

## Sea-Arama Marineworld

Linda Meyer Sivy–Snack bar, skier
Mary Jo Urbani–Skier
Mike Baxter–Marketing director
Mike Cromie–Pirates Nook snack bar,
supervisor of food services, groundskeeper
supervisor
Mike Sass–Trainer of bears, sea lions, dolphins
Mike Schultz–Trainer, dolphins, sea lions
Nick O'Donohoe–Skier
Paul Ware–Trainer, dolphins, sea lions
Paul Humason–Skier
Russell O'Connor–Director of
maintenance/operations

Russ Ware–Skier
Sharon Little Campolongo–Big cat show,
concessions
Terry Moore–Ski show director
Terry Overstreet–Live show director and
announcer
Victor Sorrento–Snake handler, curator,
maintenance, announcer, marine mammal
trainer
Yolanda Almanza Quintanilla–Concessions,
gift shop

**Some of the Animals:**
Sea Hag–blue and gold macaw arrives, three
months old
Pete–blue and gold macaw arrives, three
months old
Ivan–Siberian tiger
Ravi–Bengal tiger
Sabra–Asian leopard
Kunta–black panther
Duke–German shepherd dog
Leonard–lion
Charlie Brown–dolphin
Zsa-Zsa–dolphin

Lucky–dolphin
Connie–dolphin
Hastings–dolphin
Beta–dolphin
Alpha–dolphin
Sigma–dolphin
Big Al–dolphin
Tuna–sea lion
Duffer–sea lion
Sandy–sea lion
Aramis–sea lion
Constance–sea lion
Barnaby–seal
Whitie–seal
Blackie–seal

# 1981

New for this year was the Aldabra land tortoises' habitat, made of stone and timbers. Its rustic appearance fit in nicely with the surrounding palms and oleanders. Other improvements in 1981 included placing the U.S. and Sea-Arama flags at the front entrance, remodeling the front gate area, completing some additional landscaping, and installing better sound systems.

In April visitors could see the exciting new shark show. New types of larger, more aggressive sharks were added to the existing 15 specimens in the Oceanarium. The aluminum shark cage was introduced due to the possible danger of working with these potential killers.

The Jungle Fantasy Wild Cat Show ended its run at Sea-Arama in May of this year.

The park introduced another costumed character called Cap'n Sharkey, and the week of April 17–19 was proclaimed Cap'n Sharkey Weekend. During that time the character gave away a free stuffed animal to each of the first 200 children to enter the park.

Over the past few years, the park's Educational Services Department had taken on a larger role. The department was responsible for the hundreds of students who visited the park on class outings and field trips. It also provided everything from printed materials on dolphins and sharks to full-color graphics and posters. In addition, the park published a weekly newspaper column for children called Fishy Facts for Children. This department served as a major player in Sea-Arama's outreach programs.

Sea-Arama's research work continued this year. Efforts included developing a local nesting area for the endangered brown pelican, studying the Ridley sea turtle, and exploring the effects of certain stimuli on sharks.

On August 31, a pygmy sperm whale was brought to Sea-Arama. It had beached itself on Padre Island after receiving a gunshot wound behind the dorsal fin. Unfortunately, the treatment it received didn't help. It died the next morning.

John Campolongo with tigers. *Courtesy of Sharon Campolongo.*

Sea-Arama employee Mike Cromie and costumed character. *Courtesy of Mike Cromie.*

Cap'n Sharkey. *Courtesy of Russ O'Connor.*

Tim Gould

Shark in the Oceanarium with diver cage.
*Courtesy of Greg May.*

Kim Piel Conner, Kent Dodge, Linda Meyer Sivy, Bruce Staples, ca. 1981. *Courtesy of Tim Cromie.*

Skiers Julie Brown, Kim Piel Conner, Kelly Farmer, ca. 1981. *Courtesy of Tim Cromie.*

Kim Piel Conner, Julie Brown, Kelly Farmer, Terry Moore, Kent Dodge, Bruce Staples, ca. 1981. *Courtesy of Tim Cromie.*

**Some of the employees:**
Alice Law–Public relations, front gate supervisor, assistant accountant
Amber Jinkins Shelley–Birds
Augustine (Auggie) Almanza–Aquarium maintenance
Becky Russell–Janitor, food service cashier
Bob Ford–Announcer
Bob Milgore–Curator, part-time snake show
Bruce Staples–Skier
Craig Janek–Skier
Debbie ?–Concessions
Debby Chambers–Administrative assistant to general manager, guest relations
Debbie Marr–Trainer
Donna Johnson Smith–Mermaid, bird shows, animal costumes
Greg Samford–Janitor, landscaping, maintenance
Jesse Urquiaga–Food court, concessions, gift shop
John Newell–Chief trainer
John Kerivan–Head curator of animal health and husbandry
Julie Brown–Skier
Kelly Farmer–Skier
Kelley Grush–Announcer, bird trainer, dolphin trainer
Ken Beggs–Director of training, curator of animals

Kent Dodge–Skier
Kim Piel Conner–Skier
Linda Meyer Sivy–Snack bar, skier
Mary Jane Brown–Concessions at Shark Encounter
Mary Jo Urbani–Skier
Mike Baxter–Marketing director
Mike Cromie–Pirates Nook snack bar, supervisor of food services, groundskeeper supervisor
Nick O'Donohoe–Skier
Paul Ware–Summer trainer for dolphin, sea lions
Peggy ?–Concessions
Ralph McPheeters–Manager of Sea-Arama
Russell O'Connor–Director of maintenance/operations
Russ Ware–Skier
Shari Galit–Bird show
Tim Cromie–Food, gift shop manager, warehouse, assistant general manager
Terry Moore–Ski show director
Terry Overstreet–Live Show director and announcer
Vicki Caldera Charles–Accounting, galley
Victor Sorrento–Snake handler, curator, maintenance, announcer, marine mammal trainer

**Some of the Animals:**
Charlie Brown, Connie, Lucky–dolphin
Hastings, Beta, Alpha, Sigma–dolphin
Big Al–dolphin
Samson the sea lion pup—rescued from CA
Tuna, Jones, Duffer–sea lion
Sandy, Aramis, Bart–sea lion
Zach, Samson, Constance–sea lion
Barnaby, Whitie, Blackie–seal

Ravi–Bengal tiger
Sabra–Asian leopard
Kunta–black panther
Duke–German shepherd dog
Leonard–lion
Ivan–Siberian tiger
Sharks
Aldabra tortoises
Ridley sea turtles
Brown pelicans

# 1982

Very little was new this year in terms of animals and exhibits, but the park did undergo some changes in other areas. A newly designed front gate complex made the entry bridge much wider. This change accommodated the new information center that provided facts and brochures about Galveston's other attractions. In addition, fences were updated and replaced, ten black swans were added to the front lagoon, sidewalks were installed, flags were raised, and improvements were made to the garden area.

This year's focus was on the Shark Show Adventure, which featured more than 20 bull, lemon, and nurse sharks circling the diver while he was in his cage. Guests could interact with the diver via his two-way communication system, thus fulfilling the advertising of "Sea Monsters Daily."

The 1982 live show package offered six different shows: water skiers performing to the surfing sounds of the '60s, Sea-Arama's two sea lions performing in the soap operas "As the Marineworld Turns" and "All My Sea Lions," dolphins showing off their behaviors in the Marineworld Revue, snake handlers risking their lives in the thrilling snake show, and Captain Harvey trying to rescue a fair maiden from the evil villain in the exotic bird show.

Along with the shows, visitors could view a number of educational exhibits, including the Seven Seas Tour, Amazon Grotto, Oceanarium and jewel tanks, alligator habitat, Aldabra land tortoise habitat, and wild bird display, with its roseate spoonbills and endangered brown pelicans. African pygmy goats inhabited a display that was designed to be similar to their original "Dark Continent" home.

Among the few new animals in 1982 was the otter family, introduced in June. The old dolphin petting pool was remodeled for this new display, which featured a play area, pools, and tunnels similar to their natural habitat. It was the only exhibit of its kind within 125 miles of Galveston.

The only other new animal exhibits were three new tanks in the Oceanarium. One was a 1,000-gallon aquarium that featured several varieties of fish common to the Caribbean reefs and Florida Keys. A second tank contained three large flounders from the Gulf Coast, and the third held a moray eel nearly five feet in length.

This year Sea-Arama joined the American Association of Zoological Parks and Aquariums.

Robin Lusby Schaefer welcomes a newborn duckling to the Sea-Arama family. *Courtesy of Krystal Knutson.*

1982 Sea-Arama brochure. *Author's collection.*

## Remarkable entertainment at reasonable prices...

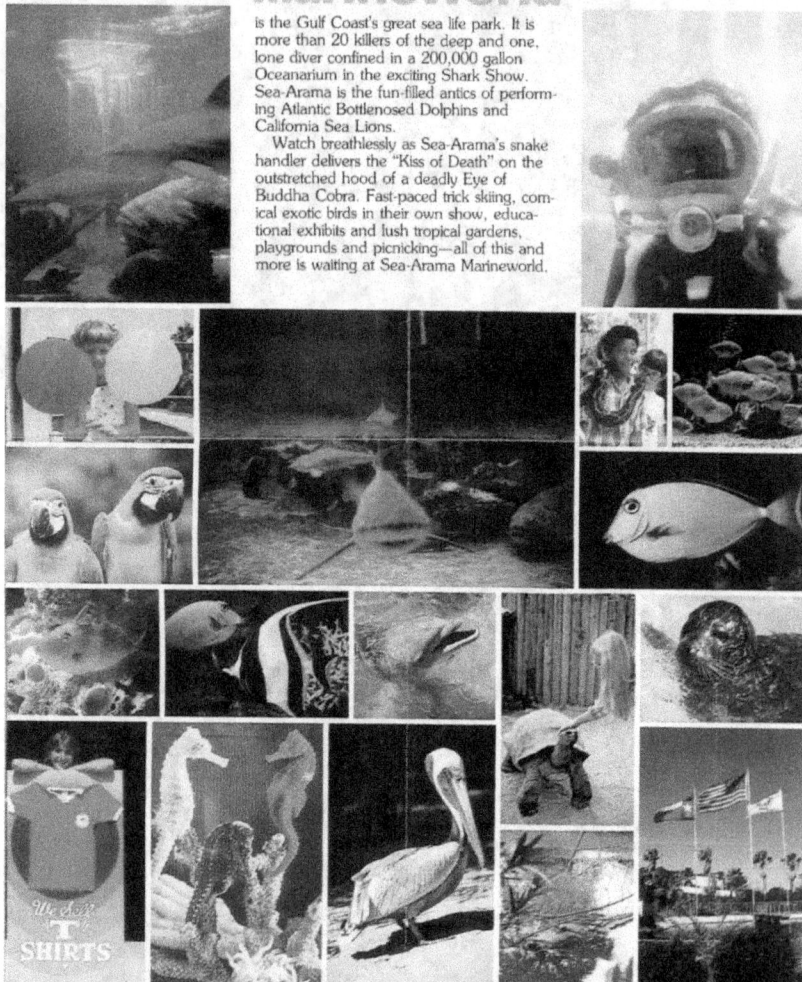

### Sea-Arama marineworld

is the Gulf Coast's great sea life park. It is more than 20 killers of the deep and one, lone diver confined in a 200,000 gallon Oceanarium in the exciting Shark Show. Sea-Arama is the fun-filled antics of performing Atlantic Bottlenosed Dolphins and California Sea Lions.

Watch breathlessly as Sea-Arama's snake handler delivers the "Kiss of Death" on the outstretched hood of a deadly Eye of Buddha Cobra. Fast-paced trick skiing, comical exotic birds in their own show, educational exhibits and lush tropical gardens, playgrounds and picnicking—all of this and more is waiting at Sea-Arama Marineworld.

1982 Sea-Arama brochure. *Author's collection.*

**Some of the employees:**
Alice Law–Public relations, front gate supervisor, assistant accountant
Amy Ellison–Skier
Augustine (Auggie) Almanza–Aquarium maintenance
Bertrand Isles–Groundskeeper
Brent Walker–Groundskeeper
Christy Benson–Public relations director
Cindy Timms–Gift shop, concessions
Craig Janek–Skier
Deanna Ware Walton–Skier
Debby Chambers–Administrative assistant to general manager, guest relations
Debbie Marr –Trainer
Greg Samford–Janitor, landscaping, maintenance
James Norris–Galley food court
Jesse Urquiaga–Food court, concessions, gift shop
John Kerivan–Head curator of animal health and husbandry
Kelley Grush–Announcer, bird trainer, dolphin trainer
Ken Beggs–Director of training, curator of animals
Kent Dodge–Skier
Kim Piel Conner–Skier
Larry Bolton–Galley food court

Linda Meyer Sivy–Snack bar, skier
Lisa Emmite–Galley food court
Mary Jo Urbani–Skier
Michelle Pamplin–Galley food court
Mike Baxter–Marketing director
Mike Cromie–Pirates Nook snack bar, supervisor of food services, groundskeeper supervisor
Nathan Jackson–Galley food court
Robin Lusby Schaefer
Roy Drinnen–Assistant curator of fish
Russell O'Connor–Director of maintenance/operations
Russ Ware–Skier
Sheryl Hoff–Galley food court
Sibyl Bodamer–Curator of 158 birds, and bird shows
Tim Cromie–Food, gift shop manager, warehouse, assistant general manager
Terry Moore–Ski show director
Terry Overstreet–Live show director and announcer
Vicki Caldera Charles–Accounting, galley
Victor Sorrento–Snake handler, curator, maintenance, announcer, marine mammal trainer

**Some of the Animals:**
Charlie Brown, Connie, Lucky–dolphin
Hastings, Beta, Alpha–dolphin
Sigma, Big Al–dolphin
Tuna, Jones, Duffer, Sandy–sea lion
Aramis, Bart, Zach–sea lion
Samson–sea lion
Constance–sea lion
Barnaby–seal

Whitie–seal
Blackie–seal
Flounders
Moray eel
Exotic birds
Sharks
African pygmy goats
Roseate spoonbills
Brown pelicans
Otters

# 1983

This year the Marine Mammal Stranding Network appointed Sea-Arama as the rescue center for stranded and injured marine mammals.

On August 15, Hurricane Alicia hit Galveston and did extensive damage to Sea-Arama. Many of the buildings sustained severe roof damage, including the Oceanarium, the ski stadium, the administration offices, and the front gate area. The ski show's sound booth was virtually destroyed by the winds and rain. All over the park the sound cables were ruined, and all had to be replaced. High winds forced rain into the administration offices, leaving wet carpet, furniture, files, and tickets. The landscaping didn't fare any better—the 100 mph winds uprooted many oleander bushes and palm trees. Several of the park's employees, contractors, and friends stayed at Sea-Arama throughout the hurricane to help the animals in whatever way they could. In the end, only one roseate spoonbill died because of the storm.

After it was over, park employees and contractors worked swiftly to restore the water quality, clean up and repair the damage, and care for the animals. Auxiliary generators provided power to the park until outside sources of power were restored. All of this was done as quickly as possible so Sea-Arama could return to daily operations. By August 26— less than two weeks after the hurricane hit—Sea-Arama's shows and attractions were up and running again.

The jewel tank aquarium displays underwent an extensive redesign and remodeling, with 18 new tanks added. That brought the total to 40, which gave the park one of the largest aquarium collections in the U.S. Each new tank display was designed to closely resemble the fishes' original habitat. Gulf Coast fish were placed in a new 850-gallon tank that looked like a pier, with visitors viewing the display from beneath the water. Another tank held a mock drilling platform and exhibited plants and animals that would naturally be seen around an off-shore oil rig.

Other new Oceanarium exhibits included an octopus and seahorse display, exotic shrimp, crabs, an Indo-Pacific section featuring unusual fish from Australia and Hawaii, and venomous fish.

Blue and gold macaw on roller skates.
*Courtesy of Russ O'Connor.*

Hurricane Alicia clean-up team, including Jesse Eliaz, Darrell Charles, Sheryl Hoff Gonzalez, Michele Falk Hay, Janell Buckner, Bert Isles, Mike Cromie, Ritch Perkins, Phillip Gilliam. *Courtesy of Tim Cromie.*

**Some of the employees:**

Alice Law–Public relations, front gate supervisor, assistant accountant
Amy Ellison–Skier
Augustine (Auggie) Almanza–Aquarium maintenance
Bertrand Isles–Groundskeeper
Brent Walker–Groundskeeper
Christy Benson–Public relations director
Cindy Timms–Gift shop, concessions
Craig Janek–Skier
Darrell Charles–Skier, maintenance, pump man
Deanna Ware Walton–Skier
Debby Chambers-Administrative assistant to general manager, guest relations
Debbie Marr–Trainer
Doug Lawrence–Announcer
George Stretch–Diver, curator
Hugh Purgley–Aquarium exhibits
James Norris–Galley food court
Janell Buckner
Jesse Eliaz–Groundskeeper
Jesse Urquiaga–Food court, concessions, gift shop
John Kerivan–Head curator of animal health and husbandry
Kelley Grush–Announcer, bird trainer, dolphin training
Ken Beggs–Director of training, curator of animals
Ken Ramirez–Show director, narrator

Kent Dodge–Skier
Larry Bolton–Galley food court
Lisa Emmite–Galley food court
Mary Jo Urbani–Skier
Michele Falk Hay–Tiki concessions, ticket booth, ski show rope girl
Michelle Pamplin–Galley food court
Mike Baxter?–Marketing director
Mike Cromie–Pirates Nook snack bar, supervisor of food services, groundskeeper supervisor
Nathan Jackson–Galley food court
Phillip Gilliam
Ritch Perkins
Roy Drinnen–Assistant curator of fish
Russell O'Connor–Director of maintenance/operations
Russ Ware–Skier
Sandra Alexander–Marketing director
Sheryl Hoff Gonzalez–Galley food court
Sibyl Bodamer–Curator of 158 birds, and bird shows
Terry Moore–Ski show director
Terry Overstreet–Live shows director
Tim Cromie–Food, gift shop manager, warehouse, assistant general manager
Vicki Caldera Charles–Accounting, galley
Victor Sorrento–Snake handler, curator, maintenance, announcer, marine mammal trainer

**Some of the Animals:**

Charlie Brown, Connie, Lucky–dolphin
Hastings, Beta, Alpha–dolphin
Sigma, Big Al–dolphin
Tuna, Jones, Duffer–sea lion
Sandy, Aramis, Bart–sea lion
Zach, Samson, Constance–sea lion
Barnaby, White–seal

Black swans
River otters
African pygmy goats
Brown pelicans
Ridley sea turtles
Exotic birds
Seahorses
Crabs
Exotic shrimp

# 1984

In September of 1984, Galveston Marine Aquarium Incorporated sold Sea-Arama for approximately $6 million to two Galveston real estate brokers: William Cherry and Kenneth Shelton. Cherry and Shelton later reported spending close to $2 million on park improvements and increasing the park's income by 20 percent per year.

Skiers Amy Ellison, Camille Prinze, Ronnie Rouse, Darrell Charles, Russ Ware. *Courtesy of Kelli Jones.*

One jumps over two in the ski show. *Courtesy of Kelli Jones.*

Skiers Camille Prinze, and Amy Ellison. *Courtesy of Kelli Jones.*

Tower hoop jump. *Courtesy of Kelli Jones.*

Dolphins dancing cheek to cheek. *Courtesy of Kelli Jones.*

Tower fish jump. *Courtesy of Kelli Jones.*          High hurdle jump. *Courtesy of Kelli Jones.*

Dolphins jump the hurdles. *Courtesy of Kelli Jones.*

Ball jump. *Courtesy of Kelli Jones.*

Ring of fire jump. *Courtesy of Kelli Jones.*

Sea-Arama Marineworld

**Some of the employees:**

Amy Ellison–Skier
Bertrand Isles–Groundskeeper
Brent Walker–Groundskeeper
Camille Prinze–Skier
Christian Dobelmann–Snack bar
Christy Benson–Public relations director
Craig Janek–Skier
Cynthia Popovich McEldowney–Snack bar, parking lot attendant
Darrell Charles–Skier, maintenance, pump man
Deanna Ware Walton–Skier
Debby Chambers–Administrative assistant to general manager, guest relations
Debbie Marr –Trainer
Doug Lawrence–Announcer
Doug Messinger–Trainer
George Stretch–Diver, curator
Hugh Purgley–Aquarium exhibits
James Norris–Galley food court
Jesse Eliaz–Groundskeeper
Jim Dobberstine–Diver, curator
John Kerivan–Head curator of animal health and husbandry
Kelley Grush–Announcer, bird trainer, dolphin training
Ken Ramirez–Show director, narrator, trainer, director of training
Ken Shelton–Owner
Kent Dodge–Skier

Larry Bolton–Galley food court
Lisa Emmite–Galley food court
Lynne Henson Quoyeser–Snack bar
Mark Miller–Announcer
Mary Jo Urbani–Skier
Michele Hay–Tiki Concessions, ticket booth, ski show rope girl
Michelle Pamplin–Galley food court
Mike Cromie–Pirates Nook, supervisor of food services, groundskeeper supervisor
Nathan Jackson–Galley food court
Ronnie Rouse–Skier
Roy Drinnen–Assistant curator of fish
Russell O'Connor–Director of maintenance/operations
Russ Ware–Skier
Sibyl Bodamer–Curator of 158 birds, and bird shows
Sheryl Hoff–Galley food court
Steve Lamb–Gift shop warehouse, gift shop, the Nook, Captain Sharkey
Terry Moore–Ski show director
Troy Waters–Cooking and serving at snack bar, parking lot attendant
Vicki Caldera Charles–Accounting, galley
Victor Sorrento–Snake handler, curator, maintenance, announcer, marine mammal trainer
William S. Cherry–Owner

**Some of the Animals:**

Charlie Brown, Connie, Lucky–dolphin
Hastings, Beta, Alpha–dolphin
Sigma, Big Al–dolphin
Tuna, Jones, Duffer–sea lion
Sandy, Aramis, Bart–sea lion

Zach–sea lion
Samson–sea lion
Constance–sea lion
Barnaby–seal
Whitie–seal
Exotic birds

# 1985

For many years, Sea-Arama had worked closely with and made its facilities available to research organizations wanting to learn about sea life. These organizations included Texas A&M at Galveston; Texas Marine Mammal Stranding Network; Texas Fish and Wildlife Department; and the University of Texas. Sea-Arama had many cooperative programs that were conducted with these and other sea life complexes.

By 1985 Sea-Arama was a member of the International Association for Aquatic Animal Medicine. The IAAAM was an "organization of professionals who were interested in the practice of aquatic animal medicine, teaching, research, husbandry or management." This would not be the only association that Sea-Arama joined in the 1980s; it also joined IMATA, the International Marine Animal Trainers' Association, an organization that "sought to foster communication, professionalism, and cooperation among people who served marine mammal science in training, public display, research, husbandry, conservation, and education."

Sea-Arama also participated in the American Cetacean Society of Galveston and had been involved with the American Association of Zoological Parks and Aquariums since 1982.

This year the seal and sea lion pool was remodeled to provide better viewing, and an enlarged area enabled park curators and trainers to demonstrate feeding techniques to the public.

This was the last year for the Reptile Show. The exotic bird show would exclusively take over the stadium in June. The bird show continued its seven-bird "Parrot Pirate Melodrama" with Captain Harvey, scarlet macaws, and blue and gold macaws.

Also advertised this year were the giant tortoises, river otters, alligator display, Amazon River fish (including piranha), and the Dive Show/Shark Adventure that ran three times a day.

Ken Ramirez took ownership of Entertainment Plus, which began this year to provide dolphin, sea lion, and bird shows to Sea-Arama, in addition to the narration and show production it had been providing since 1976. In later years Entertainment Plus would also provide shows to other parks around the U.S., and trainers would spend the winter months at Sea-Arama and then go with a few of the animals to a theme park during the summer to do dolphin or sea lion shows.

Blue and gold macaw in the bird show. *Courtesy of Kelli Jones.*

Bicycle racing in the bird show.
*Courtesy of Kelli Jones.*

Keith Wortman in the Reptile Show. *Courtesy of Kelli Jones.*

River otter. *Courtesy of John Masters.*

Brown pelicans. *Courtesy of John Masters.*

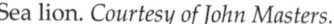

Sea lion. *Courtesy of John Masters.*

Dolphin hurdle jump. *Courtesy of the Hajare family.*

Doug Messinger. *Courtesy of John Masters.*

Dolphin front tail walk. *Courtesy of the Hajare family.*

Double baton jump. *Courtesy of John Masters.*

Volunteer petting the dolphin. *Courtesy of John Masters.*

Ken Ramirez, Mark Sweet, Doug Messinger. *Courtesy of Krystal Knutson.*

Mark Sweet as Willy Wonka. *Courtesy of Krystal Knutson.*

1985 Sea-Arama brochure. *Author's collection.*

**Some of the employees:**
Amy Ellison–Skier
April Lizotte?–Gift shop
Billy Coltzer–Skier
Christy Benson–Public relations director
Craig Janek–Skier
Darrell Charles–Skier, maintenance, pump man
Deanna Ware Walton–Skier
Debby Chambers–Administrative assistant to general manager, guest relations
Debbie Marr–Trainer
Doug Messinger–Trainer
Hugh Purgley–Aquarium exhibits
Jesse Eliaz–Groundskeeper
Jim Dobberstine–Diver, curator
John Kerivan–Head curator of animal health and husbandry
J.T. Thomas–Advertising director/park representative
Keith Wortman–Reptiles
Ken Ramirez–Show director, narrator, trainer, director of training
Ken Shelton–Owner
Kent Dodge–Skier
Mark Miller–Announcer
Mark Sweet–Trainer
Michele Hay–Tiki concessions, ticket booth, ski show rope girl
Roy Drinnen–Assistant curator of fish
Russ Ware–Skier

Russell O'Connor–Director of maintenance/operations
Sibyl Bodamer–Curator of 158 birds, and bird shows
Steve Lamb–Gift shop warehouse, gift shop, the Nook, Captain Sharkey
Victor Sorrento–Snake handler, curator, maintenance, announcer, marine mammal trainer
Terry Moore–Ski show director
William S. Cherry–Owner

**Some of the Animals:**
Charlie Brown–dolphin
Connie–dolphin
Lucky–dolphin
Hastings–dolphin
Beta–dolphin
Alpha–dolphin
Sigma–dolphin
Big Al–dolphin
Tuna–sea lion
Jones–sea lion
Duffer–sea lion
Aramis–sea lion
Bart–sea lion
Zach–sea lion
Samson–sea lion
Constance–sea lion
Barnaby–seal
Whitie–seal
Exotic birds

# 1986

In the mid-1980s the park was employing around thirty people during the winter months. By May of 1986 the park was approaching its 5.5 millionth visitor.

In 1986 Sea-Arama continued its focus on education and rescue efforts, expanding both. The Educational Services Department offered curriculum aid packets and special programs to help in teaching students. This involved "learning from animal observations, labeling, interpretive graphics, and in-depth programs supplementing the school curricula," according to the *Galveston County Daily News*.

Conan arrived at Sea-Arama this year. Conan was a 22-pound lobster caught off the coast of North Carolina and shipped to a Red Lobster restaurant in Mesquite, Texas, to be the prize in a contest. Radio station KFMK in Houston got involved and contacted the restaurant, who agreed to let the estimated 154-year-old crustacean live. The staff at Sea-Arama were listening and called in to offer him a home at the park. The lobster was moved to Sea-Arama on May 12, 1986, to live out the rest of his life, and he drew worldwide press coverage for his age and his narrow escape from death. The park named him Conan the Texas Sesquicentennial Lobster, and the mayor of Houston wrote Conan a congratulatory letter.

June 1 was a big day at Sea-Arama—the first dolphin born at the park arrived. The female calf, weighing almost 20 pounds, was the offspring of Charlie Brown (age 24) and Big Al (age 14). Sea-Arama decided to let visitors suggest names, and more than 800 entries were submitted. The park staff eliminated the inevitable suggestions related to the comic strip *Peanuts*. Even though the calf's mother's name was Charlie Brown, the trainers didn't want to start a tradition of comic strip names. Instead, they liked the comet theme of Halley because 1986 was the year to see the comet. Days later, the baby appeared healthy and was swimming skin-to-skin with her mother around the show tank.

The official naming of Halley on June 11 came at the same time as sadder events occurred. Conan had died from the stress of shedding his shell. He was buried in a flower patch near the North American river otter display but was remembered by staff and the public alike for many years after.

During the summer of 1986, the park opened at 10 a.m. and closed according to show schedules. Admission for children 4–12 was $5.95, adults paid $8.99 + tax, children under 4 were free, and admission for senior citizens was $5.95. There was no charge for parking. Shows included three daily performances highlighting dolphins and sea-lions. The two alternating dolphin shows were "The Sights and Sounds of Galveston" and "Dolphin Dimensions." The sea lion show was called "The Case of the Missing Sea Lion." An audience favorite this year was the kiss between the sea lion and dolphin during the sea lion show. There was also an exotic bird show, ski show, and shark adventure show.

In August of 1986 the partnership that owned Sea-Arama revealed a ten-year plan to spend $100 million in park improvements. These improvements included construction of four hotels with 800 rooms and a recreational complex on 25 acres next to the marine park. Approximately $1.5 million of the $100 million would be spent on park improvements. The hotels would line the man-made lakes already existing at Sea-Arama, and the owners hoped to start construction on the first hotel within a year. The lakes would be made into saltwater swimming pools, and guests would be able to take a tram to Moody Gardens, another entertainment center on Galveston Island.

The partnership reportedly wanted to sell Sea-Arama eventually. They already had a potential buyer in the Wrather Corporation.

On November 12, a foreclosure notice was filed against the current owners for default of payment on a promissory note to the original owners. Sea-Arama closed its doors in foreclosure and placed a marquee that said, "Closed for Renovation." During this time an indoor stage was built for the winter bird shows.

Seventeen employees were laid off after the park closed, leaving just fourteen to take care of the park and the animals. Sea-Arama Marineworld was scheduled to be auctioned off at the Galveston County Courthouse on December 2, 1986, as no resolution could be achieved between the current and former owners. However, a last-minute agreement kept the park from being auctioned off. Two of the park's original owners, J.K. Dismukes and Henry Ramsey, agreed to buy back Sea-Arama from William Cherry and Kenneth Shelton Jr.

Dismukes and Ramsey agreed to form a new corporation to operate the park, and twenty acres of undeveloped land to the south of the park were transferred to Marine Investors Inc.

The park re-opened on December 5, 1986, and some of the seventeen employees who had been laid off were rehired. A full schedule of shows, including a special holiday dolphin show, kicked off the re-opening.

Dolphin–sea lion kiss during the sea lion show. *Author's collection.*

Blue and gold macaws Sea Hag and Pete in the bird show. *Courtesy of Russ O'Connor.*

Harvey in the bird show. *Courtesy of Russ O'Connor.*

Darrell Charles holding unknown skier. *Courtesy of Russ O'Connor.*

Tail walk in the dolphin show. *Courtesy of Russ O'Connor.*

Sea lion show. *Courtesy of Russ O'Connor.*

Tim Gould

Final pose for dolphin
show. *Courtesy of Russ
O'Connor.*

Sea lion show. *Courtesy of Russ O'Connor.*

Dolphin bows.
*Courtesy of Russ
O'Connor.*

Charlie Brown and baby Halley. *Courtesy of Russ O'Connor.*

### WE HAVE A NEW BABY GIRL!

Sunday morning, June 1, 1986 at 6:08 A.M. a new baby Dolphin entered this world at SEA-ARAMA.

As our first concern is for the well-being of both the mother and child, we are going to modify our shows in the Dolphin Stadium.

We hope you will understand these temporary measures and participate in welcoming with joy the newest addition to SEA-ARAMA.

Announcement handed out to visitors. *Author's collection.*

**OFFICE OF THE MAYOR**
**CITY OF HOUSTON**
**TEXAS**

KATHRYN J. WHITMIRE
MAYOR

May 12, 1986

CONAN, THE TEXAS SESQUICENTENNIAL LOBSTER
SEA-ARAMA MARINE WORLD
Seawall Boulevard at 91st Street
Galveston, Texas 77551

Dear CONAN:

I am delighted, as Mayor of the City of Houston, to extend greetings
and cheers to you as you begin your retirement at SEA-ARAMA
MARINE WORLD.

We are pleased that so many people will now be able to visit you and
salute your 154th year to date!

Again, please accept my warmest greetings and very best wishes for
many happy safe years to come.

Sincerely,

Kathryn J. Whitmire

KJW:ceh

POST OFFICE BOX 1562 · HOUSTON, TEXAS 77251
713/222-3141

Mayoral letter to Conan the lobster, via Sea-Arama. *Author's collection.*

Sea-Arama brochure. *Author's collection.*

**Some of the employees:**
April Lizotte–Gift shop
Cheryl Snyder Messinger–Trainer
Craig Janek–Skier
Darrell Charles–Skier, maintenance, pump man
Deanna Ware Walton–Skier
Debbie Marr–Trainer
Doug Lawrence–Announcer
Doug Messinger–Trainer
Gini Brown–Public relations director
Harry Brown–Manager
Harriette Griffiths
Henry Ramsey–Owner
Hugh Purgley–Aquarium exhibits
Jeanne Cummings
Jesse Eliaz–Groundskeeper
Jim Dobberstine–Diver, curator
J.K. Dismukes–Owner
Joe Garcia
John Robert–Gift shop
John Kerivan–Head curator of animal health and husbandry
Jules Eggers Hurst–Skier
Ken Ramirez–Show director, narrator, trainer, director of training
Ken Shelton–Owner
Laurie Haviland–Trainer
Mark Miller–Announcer, dolphin/sea lion show trainer
Michele Hay–Tiki concessions, ticket booth, ski show rope girl
Roy Drinnen-Assistant curator of fish
Russ Ware –Skier
Russell O'Connor–Director of maintenance/operations
Sibyl Bodamer–Curator of 158 birds, and bird shows

Susan ?
Terry Moore–Ski show director
William S. Cherry–Owner

**Some of the Animals:**
350 specimens and 121 species in the park
Hastings, Connie, Lucky–dolphin
Halley, Charlie Brown–dolphin
Beta, Alpha, Sigma–dolphin
Big Al–dolphin
Dynamite–American alligator
Barnaby–harbor seal
Baby Huey–grouper
Tuna–sea lion
Jones–sea lion
Duffer–sea lion
Aramis–sea lion
Bart–sea lion
Zach–sea lion
Constance–sea lion
20+ sharks (bull, lemon, nurse)
Largest alligator gar in captivity (9 ft., 6 inches, 450 lbs.)
500-lb. grouper
Barnaby–seal
Whitie–seal
Casey–sea lion
Rocky–sea lion
Pete–blue and gold macaw
Little Red–scarlet macaw
Harvey–greater sulphur crested cockatoo
Sea Hag–blue and gold macaw
Ahab–military macaw
Butch–scarlet macaw
Conan–lobster
Samson–sea lion

**1987**

May 1987 produced a first in animal husbandry and research when Dr. Rae Stone inserted probes into Hastings the dolphin and used ultrasound equipment to view the clearest ever video imaging of a living dolphin's heart.

Also in May, Sea-Arama curators released two loggerhead sea turtles that had been receiving treatment after they were entangled in trash dumped in the Gulf of Mexico. The U.S. Coast Guard dropped the 100–150-pound female turtles about 25 miles offshore after they had been recovering at the park for two years. The curators at Sea-Arama surmised that the turtles weren't able to tell the difference between jellyfish, which they normally eat, and plastic. The two also got tangled up in fishing line, rope, and nets that had been discarded or lost. The park believed their full recovery would enable them to live a long life in the wild.

On August 15, tragedy struck when 11 of the park's 21 sharks died because of an electrical fire in a circuit box. The fire shut down the pumps that cleaned the sharks' tank and also destroyed the connections for emergency generators. This left the 160,000-gallon tank without a filtration system for ten hours. Ten bull sharks and one lemon shark died partially because of a buildup of waste.

By November the new SeaWorld in San Antonio was making its presence known by a rash of advertising, especially in Galveston and Houston. Sea-Arama had drawn 225,000 visitors in 1987, and management expected to lose a few customers when SeaWorld opened. But Sea-Arama officials also hoped to gain some of the out-of-state visitors their San Antonio competitor would bring to Texas.

School Announcement. *Courtesy of Gini Brown.*

OCTOBER 1, 1986 through MARCH 2, 1987
REDUCED PRICES FOR SCHOOLS
$2.75 per student (Pre-school - Grade 6)
$3.25 includes a Behind-the-Scenes tour
$5.00 per student (Grades 7-12)
$5.50 includes a Behind-the-Scenes tour
IF YOU CAN'T COME TO US . . . WE'LL COME TO YOU!
Call us and we'll give you all the details.
SEA-ARAMA MARINEWORLD . . . Education Department
409-744-4502    or    713-488-4480    OVER

Jody Rassmussen, Mike Millard, Cori Hawkins, Cheryl Snyder, Laurie Haviland, Doug Messinger, Mark Miller. *Courtesy of Mike Millard.*

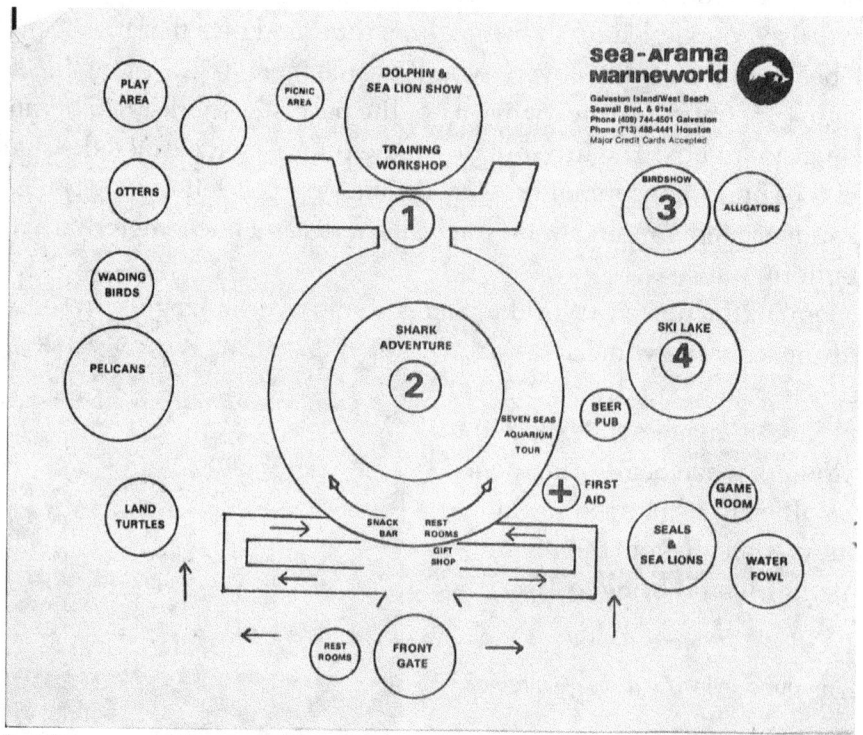

Sea-Arama map. *Courtesy of Greg May.*

## DAILY SHOW SCHEDULE

9:50 OPEN
10:00 7 SEAS TOUR ................................................................. Show Area #2
10:30 DOLPHIN SHOW .......................................................... Show Area #1
11:10 SHARK SHOW ............................................................. Show Area #2
11:40 SEA LION SHOW ........................................................ Show Area #1
12:05 LUNCH
12:30 BIRD SHOW ............................................................... Show Area #3
1:10 DOLPHIN SHOW .......................................................... Show Area #1
1:50 SHARK SHOW ............................................................. Show Area #2
2:20 SEA LION SHOW ........................................................ Show Area #1
2:45 EXHIBIT VIEWINGS
3:10 BIRD SHOW ............................................................... Show Area #3
3:50 DOLPHIN SHOW .......................................................... Show Area #1
4:30 SHARK SHOW ............................................................. Show Area #2
5:00 CLOSE

Pirate's Nook Snack Bar and Treasure Chest Gift Shop hours: 9:50 a.m. - 5:00 p.m.
Ticket Booth & Front Gate hours: 9:50 a.m. - 4:30 p.m.

** Souvenir Mug Special    Mug with soft drink - $1.25    Mug with beer $1.85 **

Sea-Arama show schedule. *Courtesy of Greg May.*

**Some of the employees:**

Cheryl Snyder Messinger–Trainer
Cori Hawkins–Trainer
Craig Janek–Skier
Deanna Ware Walton–Skier
Doug Lawrence–Announcer
Doug Messinger–Trainer
Gini Brown–Public relations
Harry Brown–Manager
Hugh Purgley–Aquarium exhibits
Jim Dobberstine–Diver, curator
Jody Rassmussen–Trainer
Joe Garcia–Groundskeeper
John Dellanara–General manager

John Kerivan–Head curator of animal health and husbandry
Jules Eggers Hurst–Skier
Laurie Haviland–Trainer
Ken Ramirez–Show director, narrator, trainer, director of training
Mark Miller–Announcer, dolphin/sea lion show trainer
Michele Hay–Take out
Mike Millard–Announcer
Rae Stone–Veterinarian
Rene Gilbert–Bird shows
Roy Drinnen–Curator of fish
Russell O'Connor–Director of maintenance/operations

Tim Gould

Sibyl Bodamer–Curator of 158 birds, and bird shows
Terry Miller–Park spokesperson

Terry Moore–Ski show director

**Some of the Animals:**
Sea Hag–blue and gold macaw
Pete–blue and gold macaw
Harvey–cockatoo (age 24)
Ahab–military macaw
Butch–scarlet macaw
Little Red–scarlet macaw
Brown pelicans
Charlie Brown–dolphin
Connie–dolphin
Lucky–dolphin
Hastings–dolphin

Beta–dolphin
Alpha–dolphin
Sigma–dolphin
Big Al–dolphin
Halley–dolphin
Tuna–sea lion
Jones–sea lion
Duffer–sea lion
Aramis–sea lion
Bart–sea lion
Zach–sea lion
Samson–sea lion
Constance–sea lion
Barnaby–harbor seal

**1988**

In March, new management stepped into place in the person of three new operating directors: Ralph McPheeters, Eugene Lucas, and John Dellanera.

This year marked the official opening of SeaWorld in Texas.

During the summer of 1988, Entertainment Plus sent two trainers, an announcer, and dolphins to Jolly Roger Amusement Park in Ocean City, Maryland, to provide shows. At the same time, two other trainers and two sea lions went to Lagoon and Pioneer Village near Salt Lake City, Utah, to provide sea lion shows to that park. All of the trainers and animals returned to Sea-Arama after the summer season was over.

In the middle of September, Hurricane Gilbert was making its way toward Galveston, and park officials made plans to move the dolphins and sea lions. There was the potential for Gilbert to become a dangerously strong hurricane, and Sea-Arama wasn't going to take any chances if it headed their way.

There were nine dolphins and fifteen sea lions to move to Texas A&M University in College Station. Even though the park contained mostly water animals, water contamination was the problem. Park officials knew the filtering system wouldn't be able to protect all the animals from bacteria that would come in from the floodwaters.

The park couldn't—and didn't need to—move all of the animals. The sharks would be okay for three or four days in the main tank as long as curators mass fed them. Their tanks were inside the Oceanarium and had a different filtering system that was better able to deal with any flooding. The birds could take care of themselves by catching their own food.

Other outdoor animals that would be okay in the storm were the river otters and alligators.

The only animals moved with trucks would be the dolphins and sea lions, which at the time were valued at $10,000–$20,000 each. The estimated cost of moving that many animals was about $6,000.

Sea-Arama was also waiting to see if the city manager was going to give a full evacuation order, in which case the park would shut down to make sure tourists got off the island as quickly as possible.

As the hurricane drew closer, the evacuation trucks remained on standby. Ultimately the officials at Sea-Arama became convinced that Hurricane Gilbert wouldn't hit them as severely as they had originally feared. In the end, no animals were evacuated, and the hurricane did not make a direct hit on Galveston Island.

Oliver the sea lion in his backstage holding tank. *Author's collection.*

Cheryl Snyder Messinger, Pam Hlavlin, and Cori Hawkins during backstage sea lion training. *Author's collection.*

Trainer Tim Gould taking Christmas pictures with Oliver the sea lion. *Author's collection.*

Trainers Pam Hlavlin and Cori Hawkins backstage at Dolphin Stadium. *Author's collection.*

Trainer Tim Gould with Hastings the dolphin taking Christmas pictures. *Author's collection.*

**Some of the employees:**
Carmen Ramirez–Bird show
Cheryl Snyder Messinger–trainer
Cherie ?–Trainer
Cori Hawkins–Trainer
Craig Janek–Skier
Craig LaMere–Trainer
Deanna Ware Walton–Skier
Donna ?–Trainer
Doug Lawrence–Announcer
Doug Messinger–Trainer
Eric Hovland–Curator of fish, diver
Eugene Lucas–Operating director
Gini Brown–Public relations
Greg Whittaker–Diver, fish tanks
Harry Brown–Manager
Hugh Purgley–Aquarium exhibits
Jim Dobberstine–Diver, curator
John Dellanera–Operating director

Jules Eggers Hurst–Skier
Ken Ramirez–Show director, narrator, trainer, director of training
Laurie Haviland–Trainer
Lancer Benson–Gift shop, snack bar
Mark Miller–Announcer, dolphin/sea lion show trainer
Mike Millard–Announcer
Pam Hlavlin–Trainer
Ralph McPheeters–Operating director
Rene Gilbert–Bird shows, trainer
Ronnie Rouse–Ski show director
Roy Drinnen–Curator of fish
Russell O'Connor–Director of maintenance/operations
Steve Martino–Announcer
Tim Gould–Trainer

**Some of the Animals:**
Duffer–sea lion
Hastings–dolphin
Lucky–dolphin
Connie–dolphin
Halley–dolphin
Alpha–dolphin
Sigma–dolphin
Beta–dolphin
Big Al–dolphin
Aramis–sea lion

Jones–sea lion
Samson–sea lion
Bart–sea lion
Zach–sea lion
Bucky–sea lion
Slick–sea lion
Oliver–sea lion
Pugsley–sea lion
Roscoe–sea lion
Elrod–sea lion
Constance–sea lion
Tuna–sea lion
Barnaby–seal
Exotic birds

# 1989

The year 1989 was filled with extreme highs and lows at Sea-Arama. There was great excitement at the birth of some animals and much sadness at the death of others.

The bright note in all these ups and downs was the new two-part dolphin show, "Dolphins: Myths and Legends."

In January, Sea-Arama loaned four male sea lions to the Houston Zoo so that the new McGovern Mammal Marina would have animals during its opening celebration. This celebration marked the end of a two-year absence of the animals from the zoo's collection. The zoo's own two seals and three sea lions would be arriving later in January because the zoo needed to clear federal permits so that all their animals could travel to their new Houston home. Trainers from Sea-Arama made the trip to the zoo to feed the loaned sea lions and do shows for the zoo audiences.

In February a baby otter was born at the North American river otter exhibit. An Australian black swan also had a new baby.

The big news on April 3 was the arrival of two young Pacific black whales to Sea-Arama Marineworld. Overall attendance and profit had been down at Sea-Arama lately, and this news presented the park's best efforts at rejuvenation. The whales had been captured in December by commercial fishermen from Japan, where whale meat is considered a delicacy. Sea-Arama purchased the whales and kept them from certain death.

The black whales were kept in a small bay to become accustomed to captivity and then put in slings in special containers for their trip to the United States. A Sea-Arama veterinarian and trainer sprayed the whales' backs with water during the trip to keep them cool. They flew from Osaka, Japan, on a 747 to Anchorage, Alaska, and then to Chicago, where they changed planes to a charted aircraft bound for Galveston.

After making the 48-hour trip by truck and airplane, the two 13-foot female whales were eating and making themselves at home in the Sea-Arama whale pool. The plan was to let them adjust and then allow them to move from the whale pool to the stadium pool. They would be put on display for public viewing after a few days and would be named within the next week. Eventually, they would have a part in a show.

On April 11 a three-day-old dolphin calf at Sea-Arama died of unknown causes. The mother was Sigma, a 16-year-old dolphin that had been at Sea-Arama since 1975. Trainers thought maybe the death of the baby was caused by an inability to fight off a natural toxin. Trainers explained to the media that the first month of life is very critical for a newborn as they can be susceptible to natural bacteria.

The calf and mother had been under 24-hour watch by the trainers when the calf suddenly quit swimming and sank. The baby was at the bottom of the pool and didn't come up for air. Sigma tried to push the baby to the surface, but it didn't work. It was a big surprise and upsetting for the trainers, who had seen the baby nursing and thought it was healthy.

Another dolphin at Sea-Arama, 16-year-old Beta, was expecting a baby in May or June.

This year the park opened daily at 10 a.m. The shows included "Dolphins–Myths & Legends," "Case of the Missing Sea Lion," "Shark Adventure," "Exotic Bird Show," and "Hillbilly Water Ski Show."

May 3 brought more sad news when Nami, one of the two Pacific black whales, died. Trainers were making regular checks on both whales and on the water conditions and noticed Nami having trouble breathing and swimming. Trainers jumped into the water to try to help, but she died 10 minutes later. It was an emotional and scary time for the trainers as it was unexpected. Both whales had recently begun to take food out of the trainers' hands. The other whale, Tanoshi, swam by herself, appearing to be okay. Later on, an autopsy of the six-year-old Nami showed tumors throughout her body.

On May 18, Beta, the pregnant 16-year-old dolphin, had her first baby. It lived only until June 13, even though trainers kept a 24-hour watch to make sure everything was okay. An initial necropsy, or autopsy, of the dolphin calf's body revealed no signs of illness or injury.

September 2 saw a 900-pound baby sperm whale beached west of Sabine Pass, Texas. The baby was only a few weeks old and lay in the shallow waters until rescuers came. They rubbed zinc oxide on its skin to protect it from the sun, and then the whale was loaded onto a foam-covered flatbed truck and escorted by police to Sea-Arama. The 12-foot whale was then placed under observation, care, and feeding on a 24-hour watch schedule that included trainers and volunteers from the Marine Mammal Stranding Network. He was named Odie by Sea-Arama staff and received local and national media attention. He was thought to be the first of his kind brought into captivity. Sperm whales are the largest of the toothed whale family, growing up to 60 feet.

Marine mammal experts surmised that Odie's outward appearance looked good and that possibly he suffered some internal illness that took him from his mother. A baby sperm whale will nurse for up to six months, and Odie had not even cut his teeth yet. No one knew exactly what or how to feed the baby, so he was fed fluids through a tube that trainers put in his mouth to his stomach. Trainers and volunteers from the Marine Mammal Stranding Network monitored Odie around the clock, keeping track of everything he did.

On September 10, barely a week after being rescued, Odie the baby sperm whale died. Because of the time and effort put in to save him, an emotional bond had been created, and all involved were saddened by his passing.

Some of the baby's organs were preserved for scientific study, and experts at Texas A&M University attempted to determine his cause of death. No immediate causes were found.

On September 19 a baby dolphin was found stranded on a Port Aransas beach and taken to Sea-Arama, where it died on September 26. Studies later showed the baby, named Oxy by the staff, was overwhelmed by parasites and infection.

Sea-Arama was closed on October 16 and 17 because of minor damage caused by Hurricane Jerry, which had swept through the Gulf on October 15.

Dolphins Alpha, Connie, Lucky, Hastings, and baby Halley. *Author's collection.*

Connie the dolphin doing her "Texas Tornado" during the dolphin show. *Author's collection.*

Doug Messinger with Lucky and Hastings doing the foot push out of the water. *Author's collection.*

Tim Gould and sea lions Constance & Tuna during sea lion feeding. *Author's collection.*

Tim Gould with Constance and Tuna. *Author's collection.*

Sammy the sea lion with Tim Gould and announcer Becky during sea lion show. *Author's collection.*

Sammy the sea lion and Lucky the dolphin kissing during the sea lion show. *Author's collection.*

Tim Gould and Sea
Hag the blue and gold
macaw during a
training session.
*Author's collection.*

Tim Gould and Pete the blue and gold
macaw backstage. *Author's collection.*

Tim Gould and sea lion Oliver
during backstage training session.
*Author's collection.*

Tim Gould moves birds to the show area. *Author's collection.*

Tim Gould preparing for the bird show. *Author's collection.*

Arriving Pacific black whales (note the white zinc oxide on them). Front Row: Greg Whittaker, Ken Ramirez, Laurie Haviland, Craig LaMere, Doug Messinger, Cheryl Snyder Messinger. Back Row: Unknown. *Author's collection.*

Rene Gilbert, Cori Hawkins, Tim Gould. *Author's collection.*

Tanoshi the Pacific black whale. *Author's collection.*

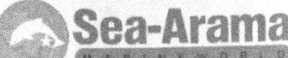

West Beach
Seawall Blvd. & 91st
Galveston Island, Texas 77552
(409) 744-4501
From Houston 488-4441

Sea-Arama is open every day except
Christmas and Christmas Eve. Hours
between Memorial Day and Labor Day are
from 10:00 a.m. to 7:30 p.m. Free parking.

Group rates available. Contact Group Sales
Department, Sea-Arama Marineworld, P.O.
Box 3068, Galveston, TX 77552, or telephone number listed above. Children under
3 free when accompanied by parent.
Reduced rates for children 3 to 12. Major
credit cards accepted.

Sea-Arama Marineworld is the perfect treat
for birthday parties and company picnics!

All prices, shows and operating hours are
subject to change.

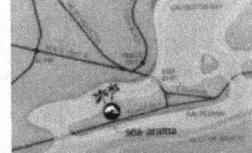

## Sea-Arama
### MARINEWORLD
### Galveston Island, Texas

WHALE!
WHALE!
WHALE!
WHALE!
WHALE!
WHALE!
WHALE!

## Close to home, yet worlds away!

### Sea-Arama

**C**elebrating our 24th season,
Sea-Arama Marineworld is the Gulf
Coast's premiere marine life park,
filled to the brim with more fun and
excitement than you can shake a
"flipper" at! And, now the adventure
is even bigger than ever before . . .
*a whole lot bigger!*

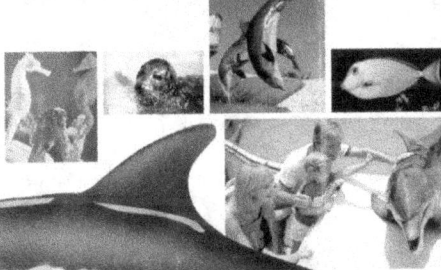

# Sea Our New Whale

**T**his season you'll have a "whale of a time" with Sea-Arama's new Pacific Black Whale; a one-ton lady like no other in Texas. You can actually see how the park's trainers teach this black beauty to perform amazing feats of marine magic. There's nothing else like her for miles around.

Sea-Arama's dolphins always steal the show when they perform with a high-flying flap of aquatic showmanship in the Marine Mammal Revue. And not to be outdone when before an audience, the park's

California Sea Lions never fail to prove that they are indeed the comedians of the sea.

At the center of this 41-acre facility is a world of both monsters and delicate, colorfully decorated sea creatures. Within Sea-Arama's 200,000-gallon ocean-arium swims a collection of "sea monsters" . . . sharks, rays, and more glide by, just inches away, watching you and waiting for their next meal. Extraordinary specimens from throughout the world fill the park's spectacular Jewel Tank aquariums.

Sea-Arama's Exotic Bird Show is always a fun-filled avian adventure! And, precision water skiing loaded with comedy and "corn" make the Water Ski Show just the thing for cool entertainment on those hot summer days.

Endangered species, giant turtles, playful river otters and more will fill out your day at Sea-Arama Marineworld, so don't miss out on Galveston's best entertainment value.

1989 brochure. *Author's collection.*

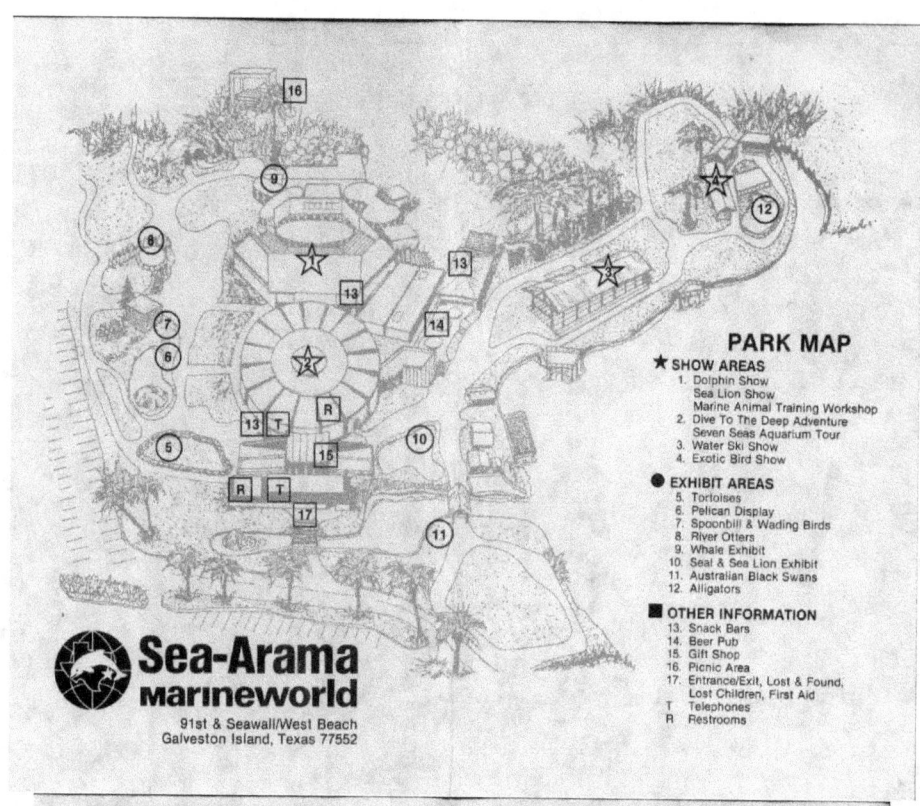

**PARK MAP**

★ **SHOW AREAS**
1. Dolphin Show
   Sea Lion Show
   Marine Animal Training Workshop
2. Dive To The Deep Adventure
   Seven Seas Aquarium Tour
3. Water Ski Show
4. Exotic Bird Show

● **EXHIBIT AREAS**
5. Tortoises
6. Pelican Display
7. Spoonbill & Wading Birds
8. River Otters
9. Whale Exhibit
10. Seal & Sea Lion Exhibit
11. Australian Black Swans
12. Alligators

■ **OTHER INFORMATION**
13. Snack Bars
14. Beer Pub
15. Gift Shop
16. Picnic Area
17. Entrance/Exit, Lost & Found,
    Lost Children, First Aid
T  Telephones
R  Restrooms

**Sea-Arama marineworld**
91st & Seawall/West Beach
Galveston Island, Texas 77552

**SHOW TIMES**

| | | |
|---|---|---|
| SEA LION SHOWS | Stadium | ★ 1 |
| 10:30 1:30 5:00 | | |
| WATER SKI SHOWS | Stadium | ★ 3 |
| 11:00 2:30 6:00 | | |
| EXOTIC BIRD SHOWS | Stadium | ★ 4 |
| 11:45 3:15 | | |
| DOLPHIN SHOWS | Stadium | ★ 1 |
| 12:15 3:45 6:45 | | |
| DIVE TO THE DEEP ADVENTURE | Stadium | ★ 2 |
| 1:00 4:30 | | |
| MARINE ANIMAL TRAINING WORKSHOP | Stadium | ★ 1 |
| 2:00 5:30 | | |
| SEVEN SEAS AQUARIUM TOUR | Stadium | ★ 2 |

10:00 (Aquariums can be viewed at any time)

**EXHIBIT FEEDINGS & PRESENTATIONS**

| | | |
|---|---|---|
| TORTOISE EXHIBIT | Area | 5 |
| 11:45 | | |
| SEA LION EXHIBIT | Area | 10 |
| 1:00 & 4:30 | | |
| PELICAN EXHIBIT | Area | 6 |
| 2:00 | | |
| RIVER OTTER EXHIBIT | Area | 8 |
| 3:15 | | |
| SPOONBILL EXHIBIT | Area | 7 |
| 5:30 | | |

PIRATES NOOK SNACK BAR and
TREASURE CHEST GIFT SHOP HOURS
9:50 A.M. to 7:30 P.M.

TICKET BOOTH AND FRONT GATE HOURS
9:50 A.M. to 7:30 P.M.

**SOUVENIR MUG SPECIAL**
MUG WITH SOFT DRINK  $1.75
MUG WITH BEER  $2.50

1989 Sea-Arama program. *Author's collection.*

**Some of the employees:**
Becky ?–Announcer
Cheryl Snyder Messinger–Senior trainer
Cori Hawkins–Trainer
Craig Janek–Skier
Craig LaMere–Trainer dolphins, sea lions, birds, Pacific black whale
Deanna Ware Walton–Skier
Doug Messinger–Supervisor of trainer
Doug Lawrence–Announcer
Eric Hovland–Curator of fish, diver
Greg Whittaker–Diver, fish tanks
Harry Brown–Manager
Jim Dobberstine–Diver, curator
Jules Eggers Hurst–Skier
Ken Ramirez–Show director, narrator, trainer, director of training
Lancer Benson–Gift shop, snack bar
Laurie Haviland–Trainer
Mark Miller–Announcer, dolphin/sea lion show trainer
Mike Millard–Announcer
Pam Hlavlin–Trainer
Rene Gilbert–Bird show
Ronnie Rouse–Ski show director
Roy Drinnen–Curator of fish
Russell O'Connor–Director of maintenance/operations
Steve Martino–Announcer
Tim Gould–Trainer

**Some of the Animals:**
Hastings–dolphin
Lucky–dolphin
Connie-dolphin
Halley–dolphin
Big Al–dolphin
Alpha–dolphin
Sigma–dolphin
Beta–dolphin
Aramis–sea lion
Jones–sea lion
Samson–sea lion
Slick–sea lion
Oliver–sea lion
Bucky–sea lion
Pugsley–sea lion
Roscoe–sea lion
Bart–sea lion
Zach–sea lion
Elrod–sea lion
Constance–sea lion
Tuna–sea lion
Nami–Pacific black whale
Tanoshi–Pacific black whale
Bucky–sea lion
Barnaby–seal
Two 500-lb. Aldabra tortoises
Barnaby–harbor seal
North American river otters
Two Pacific black whales
Exotic birds
Australian black swans
Brown pelicans
Roseate spoonbills

# 1990

By the late 1980s, Sea-Arama's facilities had begun showing signs of deterioration. A decline in attendance had been noted since the opening of SeaWorld in San Antonio in 1988. On January 5, 1990, newspaper articles reported that, due to rising costs and dropping attendance, Sea-Arama Marineworld's owners had decided to put the park up for sale or lease.

On January 14, the last shows were performed at Sea-Arama. The schedule for the first two weeks of January had included:

- Sea lion exhibit feeding and training session at 10:30
- Shark Adventure show at 11:00
- Dolphin show at 11:30
- Exotic bird show at 12:45

Most of the shows repeated twice during the day. Admission to the park in January was $10.95 for adults and $7.95 for children 3 to 12 years old.

**Some of the employees:**

Cheryl Snyder Messinger–Senior trainer
Craig LaMere–Trainer
Don Schattell–Park Board executive director
Doug Messinger–Supervisor of trainers
Doug Lawrence–Announcer
Eric Hovland–Curator of fish, diver
Gene Lucas–President, Sea-Arama Inc.
Greg Whittaker–Diver, fish tanks
Harry Brown–Manager
Jack Dismukes–Trustee of the Sea-Arama Liquidating Trust

Jim Dobberstine–Diver, curator
Ken Ramirez–Show director, narrator, trainer, director of training
Lancer Benson–Gift shop, snack bar
Laurie Haviland–Trainer
Mike Millard–Announcer
Russell O'Connor–Director of maintenance/operations

**Some of the Animals:**

Hastings–dolphin
Lucky–dolphin
Connie–dolphin
Halley–dolphin
Big Al–dolphin
Alpha–dolphin
Sigma–dolphin
Beta–dolphin
Samson–sea lion
Slick–sea lion
Oliver–sea lion

Bucky–sea lion
Pugsley–sea lion
Roscoe–sea lion
Bart–sea lion
Zach–sea lion
Elrod–sea lion
Constance–sea lion
Tuna–sea lion
Tanoshi–Pacific black whale
Bucky–sea lion
Barnaby–seal
Exotic birds

# Additional Sea-Arama Marineworld Employees

Armando Almanza–Maintenance

Amy Minneri–Skier 1980s

Andy Singer–Costumed character, ticket booth

Andy St. John–1980s

Andrew Kaldis–Skier

Angelia Marie Fridley

Betsy Wright Gregson–Mermaid, gift shop

Bill Beshears–Skier

Bob Putgnat–Snakes and reptiles

Carol Fougerousse–Skier mid to late 1970s

Cathy Carter–Skier

Cecily Wilson Henderson–Mermaid in the late '70s

Cindy Rouse–Mermaid 1970s, skier

Clyde Chubby Johnson–Alligators, diver

Dana Kovacevich–Skier

Danny Reegan–Skier

Danny Rouse–Skier

Danny Scheffler–Skier

Darlene Yvonne Berger–Concessions, gift shop

Dave Sweeny–Dolphin trainer

Debbie Fortini–Trainer, mermaid

Diane Reinarz–Gift shop

Gerry Klay–Aquarist and collector who sold to Sea-Arama

Hector Hernandez

Henry Thibodeaux–1970s

Irene Alvarado Leyva–Greeter, gift shop

Jackie Juneman–Skier late 1970s and 1980s

Jackie Rourke–Skier 1980s

Jeff Sullivan–Alligators

Jeff Westbrook--Skier

Jerry Jones–Server in Ski Shack and main restaurant

## Sea-Arama Marineworld

Jim P. Lester
Karl Decker–Drove/provided maintenance for "clown" ski boat late '70s/early '80s
Kathleen Ryder Wood–Skier
Katie Brown–Skier
Keith Cartwright–Skier
Kelly Giusti Savage
Kevin Teichman–Skier
Lennie Reegan?–Skier
Lisa Dodge–Skier in mid to late 1970s
Lisa Giusti–Skier in mid to late 1970s
Liz Whiteman Adams
Marcia–Announcer early 1980s
Mari Berend
Marlee Bisbey–Concessions
Melanie Guckian Ping–Skier
Michael Parker–Trainer in the 1960s
Mike Fairchild–Skier
Mike Haithcoat–1970s
Mike Kaldis–Skier
Miss Solis
Myra McCollum–Gift shop
Nancy Reilly–Late '70s and '80s dolphin/sea lion trainer
Orie Alvarado–Greeter
Paul Gainer
Penny Gartrell–Mermaid in the late 1970s
Phyllis Tax–Mermaid in the late 1970s
Ritchie Perkins–Groundskeeper early 1980s
Ronnie Pinola–Head cook
Sherry Schaper Peterman
Sid Steffens–Diver
Stella Musick Jares–Announcer
Stephanie Beall–Accounting, galley, Tiki, turnstiles, tickets
Stephanie Popovich
Steve Lehr
Steve Parker–Alligator wrestler
Steve Yancey–Pump man
Suzanne Tindall–Concessions
Ted McBride–Maintenance in 1970s (security guard 1982–84)
Terese Atkinson
Terry Brisco–Skier 1980s
Tessa ?–Skier
Theresa Weaks–Mermaid in late 1970s
Tony Kaldis–Skier

May 1970

# Sea-Arama Marineworld Stories

Visitors left hundreds of comments on the original "Remembering Sea-Arama" website. These are a few of the best.

### I Just Want to Sell Popcorn!

I worked for Sea-Arama in 1971. Steve O' the announcer is my cousin and I just wanted a job selling popcorn. I got hired and as I was leaving Steve said, "You can swim, right?" Turns out they didn't need a popcorn salesman but did need a mermaid. I remember when the octopus disappeared all the employees assumed the hippies on the beach got him and ate him. Then there was the day that Terry Moore and the other skiers put Alvin, the little alligator, in the girls' shower. Then there were the times we all told tourists to watch the seals carefully as they were about to lay eggs (they don't lay eggs). It was the best job I ever had.

Sherri (Peck) Aymes

### Morris the Green Moray Eel

I am the diver who was bitten by "Morris," the six-foot green moray eel in 1968. The Sea-Arama curator had told the SeaWorld staff that the seven bull sharks they were trading Sea-Arama for a pilot whale would be rounded up and waiting in a holding tank. But when the SeaWorld staff arrived, the sharks were still swimming free in the Oceanarium. So, everyone had to put on scuba gear and go into the 50-foot long, 11-foot-deep Oceanarium to herd the sharks into the holding tanks. Morris always stayed on the diver's ladder and I was holding onto the ladder because there was always a one knot current within the oceanarium to simulate real life conditions for the marine animals. With the other hand I held onto one end of a fishing net used to help corral the sharks. The sudden presence of so many divers apparently frightened Morris and he bit me on the right shoulder at the base of my neck which caused a lot of bleeding (and pain); and the rest is history!

Ross Eliason

## Bitten by an Alligator

In the 1970s, my brother-in-law worked at Sea-Arama, while he went to high school. He told me about an alligator show when the trainer was bitten by an alligator and drug toward the nearby alligator lagoon. He was able to free himself with his left hand, and as he held his mangled, bleeding right hand, he calmly announced to the stunned audience, "I'm sorry ladies and gentlemen, but that's going to conclude our show for today."

Steve Alexander

## Boy Scout Jamboree

I am not sure of the year for it was a very long time ago, but I participated in a Boy Scout Jamboree at Sea-Arama in the mid '70s. There were thousands of scouts here from all over the state and we all stayed in tents in the big grassy area next to the parking lot. There were contests and prizes plus we all had the opportunity to go behind the stages and participate in the shows. My fondest memory was being able to swim with the dolphins and handle the many birds they had there. One of my fellow scouts got bit by the macaw for he was told not to attempt to feed it and did anyway and the bird took a nice little chunk off his finger. Boy, just remembering these times makes me feel 20 years younger. I would love to see a place like SeaWorld come and revive the old Sea-Arama days for I feel it would be as great now as it was then.

Brad C. Combs

## The Place Was Awesome

I visited Sea-Arama when I was about 8. We ate at this restaurant that was right by the seawall, Fisherman's Pier or port or something like that (hey, I am 43, how clear a memory you want?). Then we went to Sea-Arama and it was great. I do remember clearly the cobra guy; Newsom I think his name was. Wrestled alligators, kissed cobras, played with rattlesnakes… To be absolutely honest I did not know the place was closed. I live in New England now and was planning a trip to Texas to inflict on my poor teenage daughter all the old "memory places." Sea-Arama was one. Google gave me the dreaded news that the place was closed. SeaWorld in San Antone ain't worth the gas. Glad this website is here!!

John Alkinson

## Tough Job :)

From 1973 to about 1980 I worked at Sea-Arama. From the day after school got out for summer to the day before school began I spent every single day there as a water skier in the ski show. I also spent or worked every night at the Bamboo Hut on the beach. It was a tough job, but somebody had to do it.

Paul Humason

### The Wax Dolphins

I remember those wax molded dolphins that you got out of the machines at the front of the park. You got to watch it being made. It was a miracle if you got home with it still in one piece!

Elaine

### Sea-Arama Song

The commercial jingle for Sea-Arama still runs through my head… a merry little tune which a young woman sang: "Sea-Arama Marineworld… la la la la la la la la laaaaa; Bring your family down for fun, in the semi-tropic sun, and you will never, never want to go home!" We visited from Houston in the early to mid-1970s. Once, I even think we went on a school field trip in the summer of 1975. It was the only water park around back then.

Julie

### Jaws Music

I always look back to the year 1980, when I was 5, and remember the trip with my parents and grandparents to Galveston. The memory that stands out the most was going to Sea-Arama. We walked down a small flight of stairs that led to a huge circular tank that held sharks, sting rays and all kinds of wonderful sea life. Although the sharks were not large I was a little leery of them. Suddenly the overhead music began to play the theme to *Jaws*. I may have been 5 but I knew what that music belonged to. I became frightened and backed into a dark corner where my mother lovingly took a picture of her freaked out child. It's funny to see that picture as well as many others that were taken. I'm so sad to find it is closed. I had really hoped to take my children there one day.

Ange

### Remember the Jewfish?

Do you remember the big jewfish in the aquarium? It was about 4' long and about 3' tall. It just rested near the bottom of the big tank and the feeders in the big diving suits would pass by and wave their offerings in front of it to be sucked in as if a big Shop-Vac were taking care of the ingestion. Also, I was there one Saturday that Hudson and Harrigan from KILT radio show were there to ride the orca. That was fun for a 5-yr. old to see. My dad was a big fan of theirs, so that made me enjoy their antics on the big whale that much more… Sure SeaWorld has all the attention for sea-life parks today, but Sea-Arama was THE BEST we ever knew in those times.

[Author's name lost]

## Bygone Days

I recall visiting Sea-Arama many times when I was a kid back in the late 1970s to mid-1980s. Every year, we'd spend at least a week in Galveston… enough time to hit all the attractions, including one of our all-time favorites, Sea-Arama. I always enjoyed the water ski shows and those red, white & blue Mastercraft ski boats. The ski girls were pretty too. A lot of other great things like the seal, dolphin and orca shows were already mentioned. At the end of the trip I'd go in the arcade and play a few rounds of "Sub Hunt" (pre-digital arcade) or get some campy little plastic or wax thing out of the vending machine—great times. I also remember those telescopes, where as a kid I always hoped to spot a big fish like a shark or a dolphin out in the Gulf. Anyhow, memories from those childhood days gone by… when the world was perfect and full of whimsy. At least there's still a little room for whimsy, right?

Gray Cooksey

## Sea-Arama 1973–1975

As a young boy in the early '70s, we lived in Galveston at an apartment complex named The Seasons just a few blocks down the seawall from Sea-Arama. The park property extended from the seawall back to Stewart St. which wasn't a very busy street back then. After school, and on many weekends, I would climb the back fence, which was mostly weeds, and make my way into the park. I watched the shows so often that I memorized the routines. The beautiful girls in the ski show were a big attraction for a pre-teen kid!! They had a segment during this time where they asked for audience members to come up and participate, and they awarded you with an oversized bronze medal with a red/white/blue ribbon. I must have collected dozens of those things! Some days, during the off-season when there were not very many visitors, I don't know how they could not have noticed the same kid was there every day, but somehow, I never got thrown out. If I recall, it was during this time that the killer whales changed—but I'm not positive about that.

Not Telling

## Terry Moore Aqua Something Team Member

What a trip down memory lane. I skied from 1979-83. Terry Moore was our ski show director. Then Ronnie Rouse. Talk about the best teenage memories of my life. Way too many memories to even begin to type. Just thinking back… Nickie O, Kent, Kim, Julie, Bill A, Cathy, Jackie, the Janek boys (Kyle & Craig), Ronnie, Kevin T., John B, and on and on. And Darrell (who could always fix/start that darn ski boat right before a show would start). What a blast. I always wanted to buy that place and turn
it into a water ski school. Maybe Tillman will call me and ask me to "just do it." I'm sure I can find someone to "pull me." Oh, the good ole days. I worked in the snack bar upstairs in

the aquarium before I started skiing. I would go watch the ski show every day on my break. Terry Moore finally came up to me one day while I was sitting in the bleachers and asked me if I wanted to ski? I had NEVER skied before in my life. I was thrilled. From that day on... I was hooked. He taught me how to water ski AT Sea-Arama. What a trip... I still live on the island and ride by every day. I can even smell the ski lake sometimes.

Linda Meyer Sivy

### A Sea-Arama Trauma

As a child in the late '60s early '70s I visited Sea-Arama several times. Well, they used to have a show (possibly the bird show) during which the actress would pretend that a seagull crapped in her eye. This was during the feeding routine, and these were wild native seagulls. The audience was situated under a covered area to keep the exposure to the real bird poo at bay. I had been seated on the bottom row with my foot out beyond the covered area, when bird poo hit my shoe. MY FRIEND DOUG AND THE ENTIRE AUDIENCE LAUGHED AT ME! This unfortunate incident has remained with me all these years affecting every moment of my life. THANKS SEA-ARAMAHOLES! (P.S. Doug is now serving a 60-yr. prison sentence).

David A.

### Former Live Show Announcer

I worked at Sea-Arama back in the early '80s before I moved back to Florida. I have many fond memories especially when I got to cover for the bird trainer for two weeks when she went on vacation and I worked 'Captain Harvey' and all the other birds. It was such a long time ago, but I still remember the opening line for the dolphin show, "Good day ladies and gentlemen and welcome to Sea-Arama Marineworld. I'm your first mate Marcia and right now I'd like everyone to stand up and wave hello to the dolphins!" How sad that no one is waving anymore. I remember 'Connie' the dolphin, extremely intelligent, and I remember how she got me on my first day. She waited until I made my entrance and then jumped and splashed—got me soaking wet! I'm sure Sea-Arama will be missed. I know I have fond memories of those days and the people I worked with.

Marcia

### Memories

I used to love the "Noah's Ark" show featuring Fat Albert the elephant seal and Rocky Raccoon. Whenever the announcer or trainer made a bad pun they played a pre-recorded track of a crowd randomly saying, "Hey now, wait a minute, come on now." Thirty years later I still mimic that track whenever I hear a bad pun. They used to blow a horn and the laughing seagulls of Galveston came flocking in for a free meal. I wanted to be in the ski show because the girls were pretty. The clown had a little red boat that wouldn't sink, even when he spun in circles and filled it with water. I remember 'Gene' the snake handler and 'gator wrestler, whose arms were scarred from rattler bites. I remember paying 25 cents to play 'Pong' on the arcade game next to the main tank and I was amazed. I remember being splashed by 'Mamuk' for the first time and being surprised by the SALT water. It never occurred to me at 11 yrs. old that the water was salty; after all, it looked like a swimming pool.

Scott

## My Grandfather

I have never been to Sea-Arama, but my Grandfather was the curator there in the '60s and '70s. He died before I was born, but I hear great stories of how he cared for the animals there. My father tells me that he rescued a sick dolphin once and he reached his arm deep into its stomach and pulled out a soda can.

Jamie McGee

## Ski Show

I don't know how many trips I made to Sea-Arama, but I have one clear memory about the ski show. See if this brings back any memories for anyone. At some point in the show, the announcer would make a comment that went something like this to someone in the crowd wearing a hat, "I think that seagull wants to buy your hat, as he just left a deposit." Always followed by laughter.

Jay Cook

## 1976–77

I worked as a curator in the seal grotto and ran over to the dolphin tank between shows. I was hired to clean the poop out of the seal areas and then thaw out the fish, place them in the prospective stainless-steel buckets, and then wrap 3 smelt in a paper towel to sell for 25 cents. We had a great time. I'm trying to remember the Manager—Ralph McPheeters may have been him. I worked with my best friend David Harris and Ellen Lindsay (petting zoo). I remember the Racing Car box in the snack bar where Tina and others worked. It seemed that was where everyone congregated after work. I also remember the little Leopard Seal 'Barnaby' or 'Barney.' I would come over the bridge and wave and he would wave back. Sammy was the great big black sea lion and he would sometimes not want to "perform" and get out into the ski lake and eat all the mullet up. Then he wasn't good for anything the rest of the day.

David Shinn

## If You Weren't There, You Missed Out

What a great site. I used to go here every summer with my Grandmother and I had a ball. I loved sharks, snakes, alligators… all that stuff. I'm surprised that I don't see many pics of the huge aquarium in the main building… the one with all the bull sharks. I remember the diver would go in there and feed the sharks and sea turtles these little squid while they played the theme from *Jaws*. One of the cooler events at the park was the snake show where this guy would do the "kiss of death" on the top of the cobra's head. I was at said Grandmother's kitchen table one morning and she brought in the newspaper and the guy had been bitten on the lip or face by the cobra. He survived but was medivacked out of the park.

Todd Clarke

## So Many Memories

My mom, Marie Long, worked there in '72 and '73. She swam with the dolphins in the big tank out back and with the fish and sharks in the aquarium. She was bitten on the thumb by a nurse shark and didn't go back in the tank after that. I remember being there as a member of the singing boys of Galveston and having my picture in the newspaper petting Mamuk. Another time when I was 11 and on a field trip with my class, the announcer for the dolphin and whale show brought out Mamuk's huge tooth brush and announced to the crowd that this was Mike Long's toothbrush! He knew from my mom that I was in the stands that day. My class never let me live that down, but it has always been a fond memory. There was a big sailboat that was sunken into the ground, just east of the main building. My dad, John, was one of three guys that I know of that refurbished it as he was a boat painter. I remember how much I loved playing the helicopter flying game in the main building and I can still smell the wax dolphin machine. The ski show was one of my favorites. I think it was Terry who is mentioned in comments here who was my favorite person there. He always treated us real nice. I remember once when he shaved his beard off and looked kinda like a clown because the rest of his face was tanned. LOL

Mike Long

## Oh Man Do I Have Memories

As a kid I grew up in Galveston just blocks away from this wonderful place. I was talking to my dad recently and he reminded me that he worked there a few years. I remember the 142' triple mast schooner sailboat too (the *Southwind*). I think I spent every free moment at that place, jumped the back fence almost every day. I know they saw us, but no one ever said anything. I guess they knew if we were there we would end up learning something. We even swam in the lake some evenings (wasn't I the devil child). I remember laying on the boat ramp and watching the stars. My kids and I spent the night in the ruins after it was abandoned and called it a camping trip. I spent the whole evening recounting my childhood memories of jumping the fence, wrapping fish for them to sell… thanks for helping me to remember those really good times.

Another Mike

## The *Southwind*

The sailboat belonged partly to Doc Rail the producer of the ski show. One 4th of July this amazing storm hit Galveston from the north with 100 mph winds and the *Southwind* took a severe beating and sank on the north wall of the Galveston Yacht Basin. It was raised and then taken to Sea-Arama. I remember it was irreparably damaged after the beating it took in the harbor before they brought it to Sea-Arama. I'm pretty sure it met its demise from the termite population at Sea-Arama. So eventually it was dismantled and trashed. I worked there from '67–'69 diving, announcing, and occasionally doing the alligator wrestling. Two big moments I remember was when the ski show first started we (divers) were told we would have to share our showers and locker rooms which were small and cramped. When we saw that there were only 3 guys and 8 girls we decided that the sacrifice was tolerable. Another big moment was when I was an announcer and Sea-Arama got cordless mics. No more getting shocked on the lips!

Ron Mozara

## Best of times… Worst of times

I worked at Sea-Arama during the last two years it was open as an aquarist/animal keeper. Learned a lot, had a lot of fun, then watched the place wither as a marine park. We tried to keep things going for about a year with some mariculture projects (after it officially closed) but that failed as well. My memories after it closed are of me living in the trainer's shack as sole caretaker for Oliver (the giant sea lion), hosting a Halloween party in the abandoned grotto (great ambiance), jumping through the broken sky lights into the oceanarium and eating fish, crabs, rattlesnakes, and even pigeon since we weren't paid for months at a time. Great fun, as close to Robinson Crusoe as one gets in 1990 Galveston. I went through the place recently and it was leveled. I picked up a few pieces of rebar as the only remaining evidence that there was anything there. The front driveway, parking lot and Ski Lake are the only recognizable landmarks. For any previous employees out there, the large low tank at the top of the dive locker stairs (carpet anemone/clownfish exhibit in '88–'90) is now the freshwater stingray holding tank at Moody Gardens. The shark cage from the Sea-Arama Oceanarium where we did the shark dive shows is on display in the Moody Gardens Aquarium Pyramid Caribbean exhibit as well… pieces of Sea-Arama live on!

Greg Whittaker

*Note from author: At the time of the 2012 Reunion, Greg was the Manager of Moody Gardens Aquarium Pyramid.*

**World Record Attempt**

I was the snake handler in 1977 and before I quit, I attempted to kiss three cobras at the same time. I had heard that someone in Florida had attempted this and failed, so naturally I just had to give it a try. About a week before I was due to leave back to college, it was finally "put up or shut up" time, so I recruited my buddy Leonard Insall with his trusty Kodak 110 Instamatic to be the official photographer. My plan was simple, get all 3 cobras to hood up in a straight line, and then I would kiss them from right to left. We cleared the snake house and here's what happened. You have no idea how hard (and dangerous) it was to get 3 cobras pissed off enough to hood up on the same table! Unfortunately, though, I couldn't get them in a straight line. However, I decided to stick with my original plan. So off I went. The results? I did the first kiss, but in spite of all our great planning, one thing Leonard and I didn't take into consideration was how long it took to advance film in those old cameras. And believe me, when you've got 3 cobras in front of you, you have to move fast! Snake kiss number 2 would have been timed right but snake number 3 turned on me and I had to beat a hasty retreat. Now snake number 1 is leaving the table. Quick change of plans... I decided to kiss snake number 3 next and then go back to number 2. It worked but there is no picture of kiss number 2. Why? Because when snake number 1 left the table he went right at Leonard. So, my photographer was a little preoccupied. Fortunately, he was able to recover in time to take a good picture of kiss number 3. Unfortunately, that's the only good picture we got! So, the attempt was successful, but with only one witness and no film documentation. I missed my chance to be in the Guinness Book of World Records, and trust me, I wasn't about to try that again!

Kevin Colston

**Many Memories**

Hello all, great website! I worked at Sea-Arama in the early 1970s and it was such a blast. I was a mermaid and swam with the dolphins, sharks and even rode on Mamuk's back. I later worked as Asst. Curator for Ken Gray, DVM. I worked there for several years with Steve O, Melissa, Jim Ketchum, Ann Trent, Jerry Foreman, Jim, Mike and so many others. It was a great time and so wonderful to have had the opportunity. Got me interested in marine mammals where I later worked with researchers in WA state studying orcas.

Paula

**Worked There While Waiting to Enter the NAVY**

My name is Rick Glover and I was on a 180-delay cache program to join the NAVY back in 1971. I went to Clear Lake City to stay with a close friend Mike and he knew a skier in the shows at Sea-Arama. Since I was already a diver, lifeguard and had worked with reptiles before, she was able to help get me a job as a diver, stand in merman (when the female

mermaids weren't available) and helped maintain the gator area and even got to wrestle alligators on occasion. We did dive feedings several times a day, according to the event schedule, with weighted hard hats and boots, a heavy set of leather gloves and a wetsuit. We carried a metal basket full of squid and simply unhooked the heavy hardhat and climbed down the ladder. We then walked around inside the tank in a counterclockwise motion (following the pump current flow). I definitely remember the huge 400 lb. grouper, along with a very large moray eel that would sometimes come out of the treasure chest located in the middle of the tank. I also remember several very large freshwater alligator gars (8 to 10 ft. long) which did fine in the salt water. The feeding wasn't as easy as we made it look like as we never fed the surface or top swimming sharks (we fed them mullet at night). All of the other fish would gang up and try to take your hand off (the leather gloves lasted about 1 week). You literally had to push big fish away and man handle some of them to keep control of the feeding (especially the nurse sharks, stingrays and big groupers). While doing this I bumped into one of the large alligator gars and it lashed out and bit me on my upper thigh/hip area. It happened so quick that I didn't know until later by some people watching that he actually picked me off the bottom of the tank and moved me about 5 ft. It was over within 2 seconds, but he left me with a one tooth scar that managed to get through over 2 layers of nylon lined quarter inch wetsuit. I still have the scar. Another time I got too close to the big grouper while feeding him some squid and he inhaled my arm all the way up to my elbow. He let me go almost immediately but not before a few of his boney teeth tore up my wetsuit. I also filled in for the Mermaid show and would deep breathe pure oxygen for a couple minutes just prior to the recorded announcer and music for the show. This would allow us to walk along the bottom of the tank with weights on for over 1 or 2 minutes. I was finally allowed, after some training from my boss, to wrestle one alligator named "Crookajaws." He was about 9 ft., had one blind eye and a healed crooked jaw which had been broken by a larger 'gator in a feeding argument. Prior to that, while mowing the inside of the 'gator pen, I had several
younger 'gators and a crocodile try to nail me, but I was able to fend them off using the lawnmower. I now work for NASA and still dive, spearfish and enjoy going to aquariums, but there will never be anything like Sea-Arama for me.

Rick Glover

### Ex-Alligator Wrestler, Diver, Snake Handler 1970–76

In the late '60s I was selling snakes to Ken Jones and in the early '70s I was at Sea-Arama selling cobras and rattlesnakes and Ken Jones had just gotten his hand bit by an alligator. I popped off and asked if he needed any part-time help, this was on Friday, and Monday I started full-time and worked there for several years. I did the snake show, alligator show, and dive show. After a few years I went to Houston, and while away from Sea-Arama was on *That's Incredible* TV show three times doing the cobra kiss of death, and on *Incredible Sunday* twice working 20 cobras at one time in a pit. Then I received a call from the Sea-Arama general manager asking me to do the shows again. I came back and took the show over for years until Ralph McPheeters became general manager. I worked, of course, with Steve O'Donohoe, who was a great announcer, Harry Blackwell, who always had a little bottle of spirits tucked away in different hiding places like the alligator ponds. Now, I still have an alligator farm north of Houston and a pest control company called Animal Control–Wildlife, Inc., and I'm still in Galveston running airboat tours in the bay in my spare time showing people the marine life, etc. I still run into people on a weekly basis that used to work at Sea-Arama. I do miss that great old park; we had some fun times there.

Hal Newsom

## Actually

It was 1976–77 and I worked there. Started out taking $1 bills and handing out "complimentary" maps in the parking lot. Then I worked at the porpoise petting pool, then assistant curator helping care for all the animals, then a stint as "Buttons" the dancing dolphin after my brother, who had been "Buttons" and had to go back to college. I loved every minute of it… well… maybe not being "Buttons" so much… But it could have been worse I guess… I could have been "Tulip" the dancing bear.

Tim Bernsen

## A Great Way to Earn $1.65 per Hour

Back in 1968, & 1969 my bride, Shirley, worked in the food concession booth. Hearing that management was looking for a part-time diver to do the aquarium show, she asked me if I wanted a part-time job making $1.65/hr. As a certified diver I was certainly qualified, but a little hesitant to get in the tank with all that marine life. Back in those days, with our first daughter on the way, we decided we could find a good use for a supplemental paycheck. I started doing the dive show, then someone urged me to try to do the alligator show, and eventually I helped with the snakes. I remember a particular exciting day when new cobras arrived. The herpetologist enlisted my help force-feeding them using a sort of caulking gun. All was fine until one of the cobras managed to get loose and we were both dodging the slithering things with the snakes on the floor doing their cobra thing, not unlike that snake scene in *Raiders of the Lost Ark*. We were up on the counters trying to keep from being bitten. Eventually, the snakes were corralled, and we finished our job but not without some grievous injury to our underwear. A very exciting memory. The worst experience was doing the dive show and fighting off the damn turtles! They were insatiable. Perhaps my greatest accomplishment was finally, after much more than a year of doing the dive show, getting the giant black sea bass, whose home was in the center of the aquarium, to take a mackerel from me. I think he knew it was my last show and made it my day. Thanks to those who must share our feelings for putting together this website.

Jay Paxson

## Mermaid

I worked there in the summer (1975?) and sometimes during school holidays as a "Mermaid." Lots of my friends were on the ski team. I still have a necklace made of shark's teeth that we picked up from the floor of the oceanarium. I remember Barnaby the harbor seal and the big male dolphin Lafitte who knocked me up against the glass in the dolphin tank the first time I got in with him. I think that was the summer that *Jaws* came out and standing at the top of the oceanarium looking down into the water at all the bull sharks swimming around, I think I could actually hear that music, the *Jaws* theme, in my head. The diver working the show tired of waiting, finally just pushed me into the water. Jumping into the oceanarium with those bull sharks was never the same after I saw the movie!

Stacy Jones

## Wish It Was Still Around

I was thinking about this the other day and I remembered how if you did not put your visor down in your car you would get a bumper sticker [of the Sea-Arama shark] on it. Wish it was still around so that my children could enjoy it as I did…

Renae

## Charles Miller

One of the things that just mesmerized me as a child in the late '60s were the souvenirs at Sea-Arama. You all remember that Sea-Arama had an alligator show, of course… but do you recall the taxidermied little alligator PIRATES that they sold in the gift shops? They were baby alligators posed in various comical positions, decked out in pirate hats and vests and cutlasses. Now, before you go all ecological on me, I would argue that the crocodilians are among the most tenacious and NOT-endangered species on Earth. I don't know the circumstances of how these Sea-Arama souvenirs were manufactured or procured; but they were hilarious folk art, ranking right along with the taxidermied bullfrogs playing musical instruments, right? Hey, I'd pay good money to find a few of those exotic Sea-Arama souvenirs; but they never surface on eBay. I'm fairly certain this is because of the low quality of preservatives used to taxidermy the animals. I mean, they basically shellacked them, right? So, they deteriorated rather rapidly. Do any photographs even exist of those alligator souvenirs?

Charles Austin Miller

## Barnaby the Harbor Seal

I saw one of the posts that mentioned Barnaby and it brought back a memory or two from my tenure there in 1977. One the animal trainers showed me the command to get Barnaby to wave his flipper, so being the sadistic guy I was, whenever I came to work and see all the kids around Barnaby's pool with their 25 cent buckets of seal munchies, I'd give a big wave (along with the command) and yell "Good Morning Barnaby!" And as trained, he would wave back. But then I had the distinct chuckle of watching 50 kids waving and yelling for Barnaby to wave at them (which of course he wouldn't), as I strolled on back to the snake hut. Ah… the cruelty of youth.

Kevin Colston

## Sailboat *Southwind* Display

In 1964, my colleague and I were crew mates aboard the sailboat *Southwind*. We were based in Antigua, West Indies, and sailed *Southwind* throughout the Caribbean. We later went our separate ways and only now, after 50 years, have reconnected and learned about Sea-Arama's connection with this boat.

Chuck Glazerman

## Good Times

I'm met with so many fond memories of good times at that place. Times I will always cherish with my family. With my daughters Janis and Carol and son Mike in tow, we would go watch their older brother Bill in a ski show and older sister Cheryl swim with the sharks. My beautiful daughter Cheryl Beshears lived a life most would envy. Wanting to be a marine biologist after finishing her senior year of high school, Cheryl started working at Sea-Arama Marineworld in 1966 selling tickets and concessions. But it was her dream to be able to swim with the sharks and other marine life. She would do anything and everything on the weekends and during the summer to be able to don her bikini and hop into the tank. She pushed and pushed until her boss eventually relented and asked me to sign a waiver because she was a minor at 17. With a little reluctance and worry, I signed the waiver because she had her heart set. Every time a shark would pass I questioned my decision, but the look on her face told me I had made the right call. One of the greatest joys of my life was watching Cheryl gracefully glide through the water while her brothers and sisters watched in awe. Though Cheryl's life ended in 1968 at the hands of a drunk driver on the seawall while on the way home from a Sea-Arama get together, we will always remember those precious family moments at a place we loved and where her dream was made. Thank you for the memories.

Austin

## Remember When

After 18 years in broadcasting, my wife and I moved to Galveston, our favorite weekend vacation spot and started looking for work. The timing was right, and I managed to talk my way into a show announcer job at Sea-Arama. At that time, Ken Ramirez' company "Entertainment Plus" provided the announcing staff for all the shows. In addition to dolphin and sea lion shows in the outdoor arena, there was the shark (feeding) show at the big indoor tank, the bird show at a smaller arena (unless bad weather drove it inside the main building), and during the summer (when most of the skiers had school vacation), the water ski show at the large man-made lake. Things didn't always go as planned. The dolphins would occasionally make their own rules and chase each other at amazing speed. While the trainers tried to get them back on script, all the announcer could do was follow Ken's rule and "say what you see." When you reached the tolerance level on that, you fell back on every interesting dolphin fact you had picked up from the trainers. During the winter, when it was 40 degrees or so and the wind was howling, we'd go through the first 5–10 minutes of the dolphin show even if there was no one in the stands. The colder it got, the fewer the visitors. Still, we almost always did the shows, even if there were only one or two Eskimos in the stands. I remember one visitor who said enviously, "Some job! You wear shorts and sandals and spend all day at an amusement park on the beach." Yeah, it was a pretty good deal.

Mike Millard

## When Squeaky Swallowed My Arm

The early days of marine mammal shows required a great deal of on-the-spot creativity in all respects, not the least of which was veterinary care. There were no full-time vets in 1966, nor were there any vets in the area who'd had a specialty in marine mammal care. We did our own treatments as best we could. When Squeaky swallowed a dowel rod, Curator Jim Kelly asked me if I'd be willing to let the dolphin "swallow" my arm. Dolphins have 3 stomachs, and if you don't get the object before it passes through the first stomach the dolphin will die. We had no tools, surgery wasn't an option, and after all, I wanted to be a vet! Lifting the big animal up into a sling suspended between two sawhorses, the other trainers positioned him so his flippers protruded through the sling for comfort. Wrapping his jaws securely in towels, turning him gently on his side, trainers Tom and Ken positioned themselves on either side, preparing to hold his jaws opened as I would gently push my arm into Squeaky's throat. He never moved and when I had pushed my entire arm in up to my shoulder, I felt and managed to grip the wooden rod. Slowly I pulled it back out of Squeaky's esophagus, then throat, into the clear, saving his life. I know that animal knew we were trying to help him, but he never even "squeaked."

Kathryn McDonald Taubert

Tim Gould

**Memories from a Dolphin Trainer**

My dream was to be a dolphin trainer. In the late 1980's I got to live my dream at Sea-Arama. The best part of the job was during the dolphin show, when I got to jump into the pool and interact with the dolphins. They pulled me around the pool, played ball with me, jumped over me, and pushed me with their nose (rostrum) on my feet around the pool and then down to the bottom of the pool before throwing me into the air above the pool to the delight of the audience. I also loved training the sea lions and was assigned two of them, Oliver and Slick. Along with another trainer, Doug Messinger, I got to go to Salt Lake City and do sea lion shows for one summer. I really enjoyed that adventure. Oliver was a huge animal, possibly 600–800 lbs. and I think I remember being told he was the largest performing sea lion at the time. The hours were long in the summer (often 12 plus hours a day), and it was no fun doing the shows in the middle of winter (see Mike Millard's memories), but it was definitely the greatest experience of my life and one I will always be thankful I got to do.

Tim Gould

# 2012 Sea-Arama Marineworld Employee Reunion

On June 29, 2012, a reunion was held for former employees (and their spouses) at Moody Gardens in Galveston, Texas. The day was proclaimed "Sea-Arama Day" by the city of Galveston. At the reunion, the Master of Ceremonies and event organizer was Tim Gould, who introduced the three main speakers, all representing different decades of employees who worked at Sea-Arama. Then the pyramid "behind the scenes" tours took place in both the Rain Forest and Aquarium pyramids. Hors d'oeuvres and a cash bar were available to everyone attending, and participants could make their way to different areas at any time to see memorabilia, pictures on a slide show, or films of Sea-Arama shows. It was the largest reunion ever done with 132 former employees attending, and it turned out to be very successful, with everyone having a great time reconnecting with former co-workers.

*Pictures with * indicate Sea-Arama employees.*

Peter Groenwold, Krystal Knutson, Tim Gould*, Steve O'Donohoe*, Jimmie Sommerfield*, Robin Rose*. *Author's collection.*

Glenda Scofelia, Greg Scofelia*, Margaret Almanza Cuellar*. *Author's collection.*

Yolanda Almanza Quintanilla*, Margaret Almanza Cuellar*. *Author's collection.*

Henry Alvarado, Irene Alvarado Leyva*, Orie Alvarado*. *Author's collection.*

Christy* and Lancer Benson*. *Author's collection.*

Diana Edwards*, Greg Samford*. *Author's collection.*

First Row: Erin Theichman, Kevin Theichman*, Sharon O'Connor, Russ O'Connor*, John Campolongo*. Second Row: ?, ?, Ray Edwards, Diana Edwards*, Kim Piel Conner*. Third Row: Mike Cromie*, Carol Cromie. *Author's collection.*

First Row: Diana Edwards*, Kim Piel Conner*, Steve Conner, Terry Moore*, Michelle Moore, Tonya Littmann. Second Row: Mike Cromie*, Carol Cromie, Tim Gould*, Kent Dodge*, ?. Third Row: Unknown. *Author's collection.*

**Admission Fee-**
Former employees $25.00
Non employees     $40.00

*"Remembering Sea-Arama"* website presents:

# Sea-Arama Employee Reunion

www.seaarama.zoomshare.com

Date: June 30, 2012

Time: 7:00pm to 11:00pm

*Location:*
*Moody Gardens Aquarium*
*One Hope Boulevard*
*Galveston, TX 77554*

Contact person:
Tim Gould
sea_arama@yahoo.com

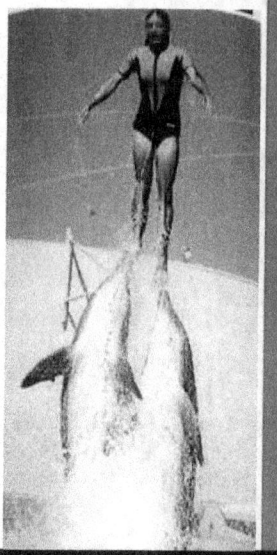

**Sea-Arama employees**– *Come join us as we gather to remember the people, animals and events of Sea-Arama Marineworld 1965-1990. Moody Gardens Aquarium will host this evening event that will include a behind the scenes tour of both the Aquarium and Rainforest Pyramids. Registration/prepayment required.*

**Admission Fee includes:**

- Behind the scenes tours of the Aquarium and the Rainforest
- H'orderves (Cash bar available but not included in admission fee)
- Sea-Arama memorabilia room (let us know if you'd like to bring items)
- Slide show of Sea-Arama from 1965-1990 (please send us your pictures)
- Other events may be included as time and availability permit

**Admission Fee-**
Former employees $25.00
Non employees     $40.00
(Fee increases by
$10.00 after 5/31/2012)

Admission fee can be paid online at www.seaarama.zoomshare.com OR By mailing check or money order made out to Tim Gould P.O. Box 580592 Houston, TX 77258

**Event created and managed by www.seaarama.zoomshare.com and hosted by Moody Gardens.**

MOODY GARDENS
GALVESTON ISLAND

2012 Sea-Arama reunion flier. *Author's collection.*

**Sea-Arama Reunion**

June 30, 2012

# Schedule of Events

| Date/Time | Event | Additional Information |
|---|---|---|
| 7:00 - 7:30pm | Registration | |
| 7:30 - 8:00pm | Welcome: 1960's - Kathryn Taubert<br>1970's - Steve O'Donohoe<br>1980's - Russ O'Connor | Location: Upper Main Atrium Area |
| 8:00 - 11:00pm | Rain Forest Pyramid Tour | Meet at Aquarium ticketing lobby.<br>Run every 20 minutes |
| 8:00 - 11:00pm | Aquarium Pyramid Tour | Meet at 1) Upper Atrium North Side, or 2) Upper Atrium South Side, or 3) Lower Level Caribbean Touch Tank Area. Every 20 minutes |

## On Going Events

| | | |
|---|---|---|
| 7:00 - 11:00pm | H'Ordorves, Cash Bar | Aquarium Pyramid, same floor as registration |
| 7:00 - 11:00pm | Memorabilia Room | Pompano Room– Aquarium lower floor |
| 7:00 - 11:00pm | Sea Arama Show Films | Oceanview Room– Aquarium lower floor |
| 7:00 - 11:00pm | Sea Arama picture slide show/Video Comments | Pompano Room– Aquarium lower floor |

## Sponsored In Part

Kleen Supply
2428 Church
Galveston, TX
77505

Remembering Sea Arama Website
www.seaarama.zoomshare.com

1 Hope Boulevard
Galveston, TX 77554

T&T Marine, Inc.
9723 Teichman Rd
Galveston, TX 77554

2012 Sea-Arama reunion schedule of events. *Author's collection.*

## 2012 Sea-Arama Reunion Attendees:

Cuellar, Margaret Almanza
Alvarado, Orie
Beall, Stephanie
Benson, Christy
Benson, Lancer
Beggs, Ken
Borsellino, Leslie
Boudreaux, Sandy
Brown, Gini
Brown, Katie
Brown, Jeff
Buff, Judith
Campolongo, John
Campolongo, Sharon
Charles, Darrell
Charles, Vicki
Chambers, Debby
Colston, Kevin
Conner, Kim
Cromie, Mike
Cromie, Tim
Cowart, Diane Flores
Decker, Karl
Dodge, Kent
Drinnen, Roy
Edwards, Diana
Edwards, Ray
Eliaz, Jesse
Eliason, Ross
Eliason, Linda
Flores, David
Gould, Tim
Gray, Kenneth
Grush, Kelley
Hay, Michele
Hernandez, Hector
Higgins, Edward
Hovland, Eric
Jackson, Hal
Klay, Kendall
Kaldis, Mike
Kamps, Susan
Knust, Susie Ahern
Leyva, Irene Alvarado

Lvens or Lucas, Gene
Littmann, Jon
Lizotte, April
Martinez, Sam
Moore, Terry
Moore, Michelle
Newsom, Hal
O'Connor, Russell
O'Donohoe, Nick
O'Donohoe, Steve
Overstreet, Terry
Picard, Howard
Pistone, Mike
Porter, Vernette Matthews
Purgley, Hugh
Quintanilla, Yolanda Almanza
Ramirez, Ken
Rose, Robin
Samford, Greg
Sanders, Judy Proctor
Scofelia, Greg
Shimek, Douglas
Sivy, Linda
Smith, Brandy
Sommerfield, Jimmie
Springer, Bryan
Staples, Bruce
Stretch, George
St. John, Robert
Taubert, Kathryn McDonald
Teichman, Kevin
Timms, Cindy
Urbani, Mary Jo
Walton, Deanna Ware
Ware, Dale
Ware, Paul
Ware, Russ
Ware, Susan
Weaver, Debra
Whittington, Pat
Whittaker, Greg
Wood, Kathleen Ryder
Yancey, Steve

# Sea-Arama Marineworld's Epilogue

When the park knew it was closing the doors, they knew the marine park's animals, including dolphins and a Pacific black whale, would be sold. The question was, what would be done with the property? At first the owners hoped to lease or sell the property for development as an educational and research aquarium.

In working toward a solution, the Galveston Park Board of Trustees formed an ad hoc committee to look into making the facilities an educational and research aquarium, possibly in cooperation with the marine science programs at Texas A&M University-Galveston. However, by early 1990, the 41-acre property and its animal performers were all put up for sale.

By the end of January 1990, three of the eight dolphins had been sold. Beta, Big Al, and Alpha were destined for the National Aquarium in Baltimore but would remain at Sea-Arama until new facilities were built for them.

The Mirage in Las Vegas was among the bidders for five of the dolphins for sale. The other two bidders were another marine park and a California broker. If the casino got the dolphins, they would live in their own area that already included a 20,000-gallon aquarium. The casino would have a marine biologist care for them and they would be used in research and educational programs for local schoolchildren. The public would be able to see the dolphins, but they would not be part of a club act.

The asking price of a dolphin in 1990 ranged from about $30,000 to $50,000, depending on the dolphin's age, health, training, and other factors.

The dolphin whose future was unclear was Lucky who had been found in a fisherman's net 12 years earlier and brought back to health at Sea-Arama. Because of Lucky's past, it would be the National Marine Fisheries Service that would decide whether he should be freed or kept in captivity. Lucky was around 16 years old and was the mascot for the Marine Mammal Stranding Network and the Adopt-a-Beach anti-litter programs. He had been on TV and in newspapers many times since arriving at Sea-Arama.

If he was released into the wild, he would have to be retrained to be able to survive, which would be difficult and expensive. The park expected the fisheries service to make a decision quickly in Lucky's case.

In February of 1990 Halley, the youngest dolphin and the one that was born at Sea-Arama, died—possibly from eating poisonous oleander leaves that were blown into her pool by high winds. Her death brought about a special inspection by officials of the National Marine Fisheries Service and the U.S. Animal and Plant Health Inspection Service, even though the park was closed to the public. The results found no critical health or safety problems.

Also, in the first part of 1990, Sea-Arama sent some of its other animals to the Texas State Aquarium in Corpus Christi. Ones like the fish and river otters were sold, but others that were endangered species were given to them. The endangered ones included roseate spoonbills, brown pelicans, and Ridley sea turtles. A couple of Sea-Arama employees were paid by the Corpus Christi facility to care for and feed the animals at Sea-Arama until their new quarters at the Texas State Aquarium were ready.

Three of the park's nine sea lions were sold to a Mississippi aquarium, but buyers for the other six sea lions and one harbor seal weren't immediately found. Sea-Arama therefore was forced to offer them for practically nothing.

By March of 1990 it was decided that Sea-Arama would be allowed to sell Lucky, and he found a new home at Arlington's Six Flags over Texas. He and three other dolphins—Connie, Hastings, and Sigma—were moved to Six Flags and began performing in their shows. The plan was to house them in Florida during the winter and then bring them back each summer to Six Flags.

The sale of the dolphins left Tanoshi, the Pacific black whale, as the last marine mammal that had to be re-homed. Several parks were interested in buying her, but first a permit from the National Marine Fisheries Service had to be obtained and this wasn't easy to do.

By May, San Antonio's SeaWorld had taken two of Sea-Arama's sharks. The park expected to have new homes for all of the animals at Sea-Arama by the end of the month. Daily discussion continued regarding turning the facility into an educational and research facility as the owners did not want it torn down, but at this time solid plans were not hashed out.

In June the National Marine Fisheries Service released 92 sea turtles back into the ocean—91 were Kemp's Ridley turtles and one was a loggerhead that had been at the park since it was found stranded. The turtles had hatched on North Padre Island in 1988 and then had been at Sea-Arama ever since in their endangered species program. They were all set free about 12 miles off of Galveston's beachfront in the Gulf of Mexico. More green sea turtles were released into the wild in August.

In July the Texas State Aquarium opened in Corpus Christi and included about a dozen endangered brown pelicans and other animals that had come from Sea-Arama.

October of 1990 found Sea-Arama hit by a storm. The park's operations director, Russ O'Connor, rode out the storm with the remaining animals. All survived, although the storm did from $15,000 to $20,000 damage to a facility that was already having trouble finding a buyer.

In December the saga of dolphins Lucky, Hastings, and Connie continued. A terrible cold front settled in over Six Flags over Texas, where the dolphins were still housed. Park officials there had heated and shielded the outdoor dolphin pool because there was no other home for them to move to. Marine mammal advocates from Dallas had contacted the National Marine Fisheries Service because they were concerned for the animals' welfare. Federal officials set a deadline of January 2, 1991, for resolution to the animals' residency problems or else they would seize the animals. Former Sea-Arama general manager John Dellanera continued to try to find a permanent home for them before the deadline.

California veterinarian and animal broker Dr. Martin Dennes had bought the dolphins from Sea-Arama but had never obtained the necessary documents that established legal rights over them. Therefore, Dr. Dennes couldn't legally move the animals to any other facility. Dellanera had offered to give Dennes his money back so he could give them to someone else, but that offer was refused. Dennes had until January 2 of 1991 to find a suitable home approved by both Dellanera and the National Marines Fisheries.

When the deadline came in January of 1991, Dennes had not been able to get the federal permits to take legal possession of the animals, so Dellanera had possession of the animals signed over to the Brookfield Zoo in Chicago. There they became part of a breeding program whose goal was to reduce the demand for capturing wild dolphins. Dennes did not get any of his estimated $100,000 refunded, and the zoo paid nothing to Dellanera for them.

One of the animals moved from Sea-Arama was the sawtooth shark named Buzz. He was moved to the Audubon Aquarium in New Orleans, and a video link on the Remembering Sea-Arama website still shows him being moved under the title "Buzz arrives at Audubon Aquarium." He eventually died January of 2005.

All of Sea-Arama's marine life eventually found homes in other facilities. Tanoshi, the Pacific black whale, went to the Navy for research on August 21, 1990, according to the Marine Mammal Inventory Report.

A plan for the facility to become a research and educational site was attempted to be carried out for several years after the park closed. However, the closest the park got to fulfilling that plan was when some of the facilities like the main aquarium, salt water mammal pools, and other places on the property were leased to local research and public education institutions.

After the facility ceased to be used for these purposes, the buildings and facilities sat deteriorating for more than fifteen years, until 2006, when the last remnants of the park were torn down.

When Hurricane Ike decimated the island in 2008, the vacant site became a debris management site. Massive amounts of hurricane-generated debris were put there until it could be moved to landfills. There was so much debris there that it was higher than the seawall and stretched in piles for acres.

In 2012, Elrod, one of the sea lions from 1989 was seen on Facebook performing at SeaWorld.

In 2016, the fate of some of the dolphins was discovered as one of the male dolphins, Big Al, renamed Akai, was still on the job at Discovery Cove Orlando. There he was riding out his retirement by swimming with visitors. Lucky and Hastings ended up at Dolphin Connections in the Florida Keys with their former trainers Doug and Cheryl Messinger. In addition, dolphin Beta, renamed Nani, was at the National Aquarium in Baltimore.

Today there isn't much evidence that a marine park existed. A careful search may find the old entrance road off of the seawall, the old parking lot, the ski lake, and even pilings in the ocean that show where the pipeline was that carried natural seawater to the park. But mostly what a visitor to the site will find is clover, a few palms, ragweed, and a variety of shrubs.

The era of Sea-Arama Marineworld is now over, but the memories, pictures, and stories will always remain and be remembered.

North American river otter exhibit after the park closed. *Courtesy of David Thibodeaux.*

Sea-Arama dolphin tanks. *Courtesy of Chance McClain.*

Sea-Arama Oceanarium in 2003. *Courtesy of Bob Ford Productions.*

Sea-Arama Oceanarium in 2003. *Courtesy of Bob Ford Productions.*

Sea-Arama Oceanarium in 2003. *Courtesy of Bob Ford Productions.*

Sea-Arama Oceanarium in 2003. *Courtesy of Bob Ford Productions.*

Location of Sea-Arama in 2016 with ski lake in the distance to the right. *Photo by the author.*

Thank you for reading *Sea-Arama Marineworld*. If you enjoyed it, please write a review on Amazon or wherever you purchased the book online.

To keep the memory of Sea-Arama Marineworld alive, print the following shark bumper sticker page, laminate it, trim off the extra, and double stick tape it to the bumper of your vehicle.

Tim Gould

# *Other Books by Tim Gould*

It was 1929, the summer before the Great Depression, and life was good. Geography teacher Curtis Gould set out on his 1927 Harley Davidson to ride around the perimeter of the U.S. His purpose was to record, photograph, and report what he saw to his students, but his adventures ended up in a magazine, newspapers, and now this book. It was a 77-day journey filled with danger, beauty, and humor—a unique time seen through the eyes of one man on his motorcycle.

The job of a fire lookout was usually an isolated and physically demanding job, living with no electricity, or running water. In the early 1900's lookouts were often staffed by schoolteachers or college students during the summer. Such was the case for Curtis E. Gould who was a teacher by trade, a mountain climbing hobbyist in his spare time, and a fire lookout in the Mt. Hood National Forest during the summers of the 1920's, 1930's and 1940's. His pictures, notes, poems and accounts give a glimpse into a profession that is quickly fading away into a past most don't remember and have never experienced.

Queen coronations, parades, and horse shows made up just a small part of what was Pioneer Days. In 1967, the small community of Lyle, Washington, began an annual Old West celebration over Memorial Day weekend that rivaled the festivities of many larger towns. This book covers each year of Lyle Pioneer Days, with over 600 pictures and descriptions of all the activities and many of the people involved. Relive the fun of the more than 60 different events, including Native American dancers, cowboy breakfasts, variety shows, motorcycle races, target shoots, arts and crafts contests, beard contests, cross country horse races, and all that was part of Lyle Pioneer Days.

www.ingramcontent.com/pod-product-compliance
Lightning Source LLC
Chambersburg PA
CBHW081821280526
45789CB00007B/2288